How to throw
the BEST KIDS' PARTY
ever

CONTENTS

INTRODUCTION

They're noisy, exciting, hard work and unpredictable – and they can be the most magical and important events in children's lives. Birthday parties are the tops, but Hallowe'en and Christmas are great fun, too. Grown-ups can also enjoy kids' parties, if they're organized with flair and creativity. And this book will help you make a party a day to remember.

The kids will be counting the days to the party, and some of that excitement can go into their share of the preparations: they can make invitations and decorations and, of course, help with all the yummy food for the party feast. Dressing up is a big part of the fun, so we've included lots of inventive costumes that aren't difficult to assemble and look sensational. There are original games to make and play, fun activities for everyone to join in on the day, and even some tricks to impress the guests.

The cake is all-important, and you'll find some stunning designs suitable for all ages. Some are simple, others more of a challenge, but detailed instructions guarantee the perfect result: your kids will be proud of you.

Preparing for the Party

While the children are bound to have lots of ideas about what sort of party they want and how they'll run it, some judicious planning on your part will mean that you have lots more time on the day to relax and enjoy it too.

Choosing a day and time
The first thing to decide is the date. This may be the birthday itself, but if you're working all week and the birthday person is at school, it's more likely to be on the nearest weekend. During the summer, you may find that lots of friends are away, so it's worth checking with the most important guests before you choose a day. Late afternoon parties are more traditional, but for young children lunchtime may be a better bet, when they're at their liveliest. Don't make the party too long.

Deciding where to hold the party
If possible, use one room for games and another for the party meal, so that you can prepare the table while the partygoers are busy elsewhere, and afterwards close the door on the mess until everyone has gone. Clear as much floor space as you can for games, stow away precious or fragile ornaments, and make sure that the room is free from sharp or unsafe objects.

How many to invite
Kids will have firm ideas about who they want at their party. A lot depends on the sort of party you are having, the age of the children and the space available, but try to make sure that the numbers don't get out of hand. If one or two guests go to a different school, they may feel lost and shy in a big crowd.

Invitations
Send out invitations in good time. You can buy invitation cards or the children can make them. If your party is going to have a theme, it's nice to design invitations that go with it. Include all the necessary details (and keep a note of the starting and finishing times, as you're bound to forget what you said). Say if it's a fancy dress (costume) party, or if you want your guests to come wearing hats, or in their pyjamas, or to bring their swimming things, for instance.

Coloured balloons, home-made birthday cards (above) and hanging decorations (right) are all essential at every party, in addition to a special birthday cake (left).

Lists

Keep a list of everyone you send invitations to, and check them off as they reply. With your child, make a list of the sort of food you're going to serve and make another list of games you could play. Then you can make your shopping list: apart from food, drinks and cake ingredients, you'll need to remember decorations, balloons and prizes.

Shopping

Large supermarkets sell nearly everything you'll need for your party. Look in your local toy shop for novelties for decorating cakes, as well as for prizes and small presents. If the children are making decorations, you'll need plenty of paper and tape, and if they are planning some outrageous costumes, they may find some stuff at second-hand shops. Armed with your lists, the shopping should be easy.

SHOPPING LIST

Decorations
Balloons
Paper tablecloth and
    napkins
Paper plates, cups and bowls
Drinking straws
Streamers and party poppers
    (for older children)
Prizes
Party bags and contents
Props for games and
    activities
Food and drinks
Food and drinks for adults
Cake board, ribbons and
    decorations
Cake candles and candle
    holders
Cake ingredients

Getting help

Managing a kids' party on your own is hard work, so enlist some extra adult help. Your partner, a helpful grandparent or one or two good friends will be able to help with taking coats, wiping up spills, working the video camera or controlling the music, while you organize the games or put all of the food on the table. Get help if you can as there will be lots to do!

Paper chains (above and right) are easy to make and lots of fun, so get the children to help out. Wrap gifts with different coloured paper (below).

Party decorations

Paper chains, streamers and balloons will help to set the party atmosphere. This is definitely something the kids will want to help with. Put a big bunch of balloons on the front gate or door so that your guests know where to find you.

The party table

Use paper plates and cups so nothing gets broken. You could also buy a plain white paper cloth and get the kids to decorate it. To avoid arguments about who sits next to the birthday person, use place cards: you can write each child's name on a plate, or perhaps draw their faces and get everyone to identify themselves.

Games, prizes and presents

If you are planning some competitive games, you'll need a stash of tiny prizes. And don't forget to get ready any props you will need for games (a thimble, a blindfold and so on). Buy small gifts to fill the inevitable party bags.

Party Themes

Children's parties tend to have a traditional format, which all partygoers pick up on at a very early age and like to follow every time. You can certainly satisfy your demanding guests by sticking to a tried and tested formula. But you can add to the fun and excitement by choosing a theme for the party. This could be suggested by a holiday, such as Easter or Hallowe'en, or it might be something that the birthday person is really enthusiastic about, such as dinosaurs.

Thinking up ideas
If you want the guests to come in fancy dress (costumes), tell them the theme on the invitations, and try to make it something that won't involve adults in weeks of sewing or vast expense. Alternatively, you could get the kids to devise their own costumes as part of the party fun: if you have a well-stocked dressing-up (dress-up) box, they can dip into that and then join in a fancy dress (costume) parade, with prizes all round. Painted faces will add the finishing touches to each costume and are easy to use.

Animals
This is an easy fancy costume theme for very young children, who can wear comfortable T-shirts and leggings and just add animal ears and tails. Older kids could make themselves animal masks. Choose an animal-shaped cake, such as a rabbit or a frog, and continue the theme by cutting out sandwiches and cookies with cutters in the shape of favourite animals.

Nursery rhymes
Either pick one rhyme as a theme or let each guest choose their favourite character to come as. These are a great source of inspiration. Make a Hickory Dickory Dock cake or one in the shape of a fairyland castle to match your theme.

Hats
Ask each child to arrive in a decorated hat, or get them all to make their own fantastic headgear at the party. Organize a parade, with a prize for the best effort or prizes for everyone.

Food
Get everyone to come dressed as a vegetable! Or as their favourite food. You could set out plain pizza bases (crusts) and let them choose and arrange their own toppings, and then cook them for the party meal.

Costumes can be easier to make than you think – a simple paper hat suggests a bunny rabbit (left) and paper wings and mask are all you need to create an owl costume (right). Make a party cake to suit your theme, such as a fairyland castle (above) for a prince or princess theme.

Pirates
This always works really well, and the costumes are easy and effective: cardboard swords, scarves and eyepatches, with striped T-shirts. If the party is in the garden (yard), you could turn a climbing frame into the ship, with old sheets for sails and pirate flags flying. Organize a treasure hunt, with plenty of chocolate coins as treasure.

Rainforest
Fancy dress (costume) ideas could include trees and flowers, as well as exotic birds and animals. Perfect for a lush summer garden, or you could create a rainforest setting with lots of green paper leaves, hanging bunches of balloons amongst them to look like tropical fruits.

Colours
Just choose your favourite colour and use it for everything, including the food. Or you could have a very sophisticated black-and-white party.

Monsters, ghosts and ghouls
All children love pretending to be monsters, and the party may get pretty noisy. Older kids will want to look their scariest, with plenty of white make-up and fake blood. Decorate the room with lots of black crêpe paper and put on some creepy music. Play some games in the dark, if you dare!

Fashion show
Mock up a catwalk down the room (a long rug will do) and when they're all in their finery – the more outrageous, the better – get them to model it. Don't forget to take lots of flashlit photographs to remember the exciting event.

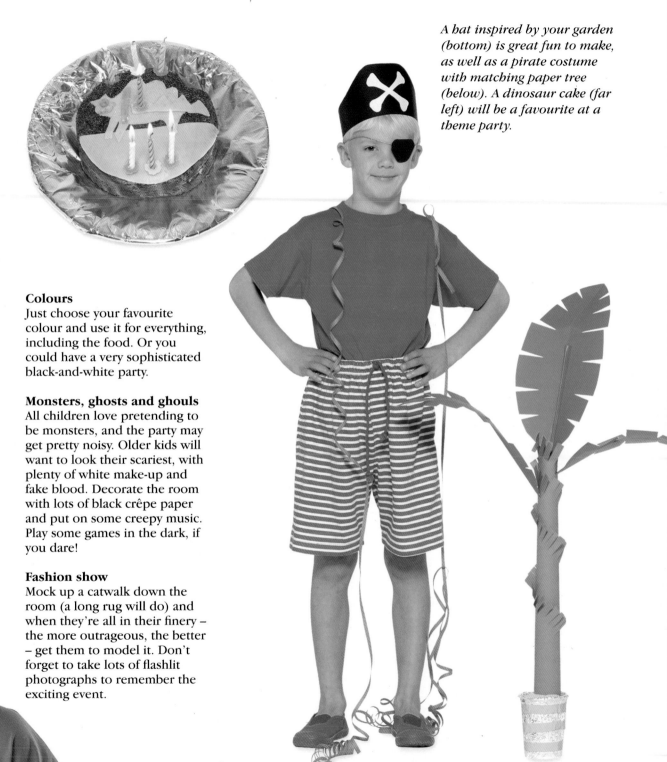

A hat inspired by your garden (bottom) is great fun to make, as well as a pirate costume with matching paper tree (below). A dinosaur cake (far left) will be a favourite at a theme party.

Fun and Games

Give your party some structure to make it go really well. Children love playing organized games, as long as you keep the atmosphere relaxed and fun. If you'd planned Musical Chairs, but they want another round of Pin the Tail on the Donkey, try to follow their moods.

Gathering ideas

It's sensible to have a few more games planned than you think you'll have time for – it doesn't matter if you don't get round to them, but it is better to be ready than to run out of ideas. Ask the children what their favourite games are. It can be fun to match some of the games to the party theme.

Jigsaw game

A good game for the beginning of the party. You can use a stack of old Christmas or birthday cards for this. Cut each one in half and distribute one set of halves all around the room (or around several rooms). Give each child one of the remaining halves to find its partner. When they come back with a pair, give them another half. The person who gets the most pairs wins.

Musical hats (*below*)

Everyone stands in a circle, all but one with a hat on. When the music starts, the hats are passed from head to head. When it stops, the player without a hat is out. Throw one hat into the middle of the circle before starting again. The last player with a hat is the winner.

Pass the parcel (*right*)

A game that is loved by young children. Wrap a prize in the middle of a huge parcel and, if you like, include a tiny prize in each layer of the wrapping. The parcel moves from player to player until the music stops, then whoever is holding it removes a layer.

Farmyard noises

One player is blindfolded and is the farmer. The others move round in a circle. When the farmer claps his or her hands, everyone stops, and the farmer points at one player, who must make the noise of an animal. The farmer has to guess who is making the noise. If right, the two players change places. If not, the farmer has to try again.

Spin the tray

Everyone sits in a circle on the floor. The first player holds a small circular tray upright on its edge and spins it in the centre of the circle. He or she calls out the name of someone else, who must catch the tray before it falls to the floor, otherwise they are out. If successful, the next player spins the tray and calls another name.

PARTY PREPARATIONS

Preparing for the party can be nearly as exciting as the event itself. There are all sorts of things you and your kids can do to make it really special and memorable, from designing original invitations to recording the whole thing on video, which the children will enjoy watching for years to come.

Home-made decorations always look great, and choosing a theme for your party will inspire you with wonderful ideas for them. In this chapter you'll find unusual gift wraps, inventive card designs and pretty paper chains, as well as stylish hats for the guests to wear. With some simple materials and lots of imagination, your kids can have weeks of fun getting ready for their big day.

Different Types of Paper

Coloured paper
Lightweight coloured paper is used for projects that involve folding, decoupage and collage amongst other techniques. Medium-weight and heavy paper are suitable for scoring, cutting, printing and folding.

Corrugated cardboard
This is often useful for making accessories for fancy dress (costume) outfits. It comes in a variety of thicknesses. Use clean, uncreased board for best results. Good sources of cardboard are discarded computer and TV boxes.

Crêpe paper
A very dry-textured, rather stretchy paper, this comes in a wide range of colours and is generally used for wrapping and sculptural effects.

Decorative corrugated card (posterboard)
Corrugated card is less heavy than the rigid corrugated cardboard used to make large cartons. It comes in various colours and its corrugations are used as a decorative feature.

Doll's house paper
Interesting papers are available for decorating doll's houses. They come in a variety of patterns including brick, stone, tile and wood and are very useful for general decorative work.

Graph paper
This is useful for scaling-up templates that are given in a reduced size.

Handmade paper
Handmade paper is made in a two-part frame called a deckle and mould. All sorts of things including seeds, plants, hair, glitter, wool, very fine thread and food colouring can be added to the pulp to make interesting textures in the paper.

Origami paper
This highly decorated, very colourful thin paper comes ready-cut into squares. It is used for making origami projects, but is also good for general decorative work and collage.

Paper ribbon
This comes tightly rolled and is unfurled to give a wide crinkly ribbon which is good for stiff bows.

Recycled paper
Now widely available, machine-made recycled paper has a texture rather like blotting paper and is very porous. It generally has an attractive speckled surface owing to the various types of paper in the pulp.

Stencil card (cardboard)
This is usually waxed to prevent it absorbing water from paint and disintegrating. Transparent plastic stencil film is also available.

Thin card (posterboard)
This comes in a range of colours and is perfect for making items such as hats and masks that will be handled frequently.

Tissue paper
Tissue paper is a very fine, thin paper that appears translucent when held to the light. It can be used in many projects and is especially good for stained-glass effects.

Tracing paper
This comes in several thicknesses and can be bought in large single sheets or in pads.

doll's house paper

tissue paper

graph paper

tracing paper

stencil card
(cardboard)

coloured paper

thin card
(posterboard)

corrugated cardboard

handmade
paper

decorative corrugated
card (posterboard)

origami paper

crêpe paper

recycled paper

paper ribbon

Folding

Paper can be folded in a variety of ways to great effect. One of the simplest methods is to fold a sheet of paper into equal sections rather like a concertina. You can hang up the finished design as a decoration.

Scoring

Scoring is a method of creating fold lines in paper so that it can be creased to appear three-dimensional. Some very elaborate effects can be achieved once you have mastered the technique. Score lines can be made with a pair of scissors or with the back of a craft knife blade. For straight lines, use a metal ruler to guide the blade.

1 Fold two sheets of paper in contrasting colours into sections approximately 2.5 cm (1 in) wide.

1 Draw the outline of your shape on heavy paper or lightweight card (posterboard). Add the fold line.

2 Fold each piece of paper in the middle to make a semi-circle. Fix the ends of the paper together with a staple.

3 Staple the two semi-circles together at the outside edges to form a circle.

2 Carefully cut out the shape. Using a pair of closed, round-ended scissors, gently score along the fold line to produce an indentation.

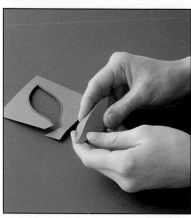

3 Gently fold the shape along the score line. Lightly re-score the line if it doesn't fold easily.

Curling

Thin strips of lightweight paper can be pulled with a pencil to create gentle curls. The curls are especially good for making false beards, moustaches, hair, fur effects and so on.

Cutting

Paper may be cut in a variety of ways to make interesting designs. Simple cut-outs are especially good for embellishing greetings cards and decorations.

1 Cut thin strips of paper approximately 1 cm (⅜ in) wide.

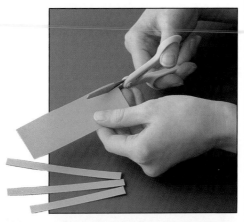

1 Fold a sheet of paper in half. Make horizontal cuts every 3–4 cm (1¼–1½ in) down the fold. Open the paper. Push every second fold backwards to make a step effect.

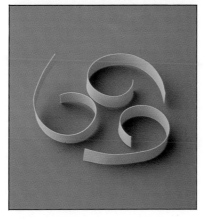

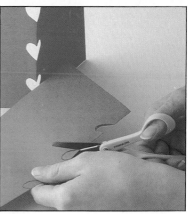

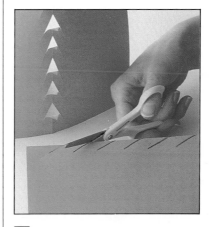

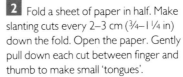

2 Holding a strip of paper in one hand, pull a pencil down its length several times. Don't pull too hard or you'll tear the paper!

3 The paper will form into gentle curls. If you want tighter curling, the strips can be rolled around the pencil.

2 Fold a sheet of paper in half. Make slanting cuts every 2–3 cm (¾–1¼ in) down the fold. Open the paper. Gently pull down each cut between finger and thumb to make small 'tongues'.

3 Fold a piece of paper in half. Cut half a heart shape at equal intervals down the fold. Open the paper to reveal complete hearts down the length of the paper.

Stencilling

Stencilling is a way of applying decoration to a surface using special card (cardboard), clear film or metal stencils. A shape is drawn onto the card, cut out, and then paint is applied over the cut-out portion of the stencil with a sponge or brush. It is possible to buy ready-cut stencils or you can make your own. You can use a stencil brush to paint your design, or try sponging it, which gives an interesting texture.

1 Cut a piece of stencil card (cardboard) and draw your design.

2 Using a craft knife, cut out the image from the stencil card.

3 Mix paint in a palette or on an old saucer. Add a little water to make a slightly sticky consistency.

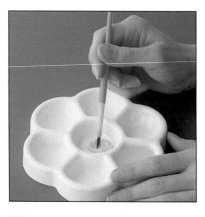

4 Cut a piece of household sponge into small squares.

5 Place the stencil card on a piece of heavy paper or thin card (posterboard). Dip the sponge in paint and gently dab it over the cut-out motif.

6 Remove the stencil card carefully, one corner at a time, to avoid smudging the paint.

Tracing

Some of the projects in this book include templates that you can copy when you are creating your paper projects. Tracing is the fastest and simplest way to transfer a template to another sheet of paper.

1 Lay a sheet of tracing paper over the template. Carefully trace over the image with a soft pencil to make a dark line.

2 Turn the tracing over. Scribble over the lines with a soft pencil.

3 Place the tracing the right way up on appropriate paper. Draw over the original lines. When the tracing is removed, the image will have been transferred.

Scaling-up

If you want to make a project larger than the template you can scale it up using graph paper. Use a scale of, say, one square on the template to two squares on the graph paper. You may use a different scale depending on the size you want.

1 If you wish to copy a template that is not printed on a grid, trace it and transfer it to graph paper. If the template you have chosen does appear on a grid, as in this book, proceed directly to step 2.

2 Using an appropriate scale, enlarge the template onto a second sheet of graph paper, copying the shape from each smaller square to the larger square.

3 Cut out the new template and transfer it to card (posterboard) or paper.

Disco Star Card and Tag

Use up your old scraps of coloured paper and cardboard to make this groovy spinning star card and matching gift tag.

YOU WILL NEED
tracing paper
pencil
scissors
coloured cardboard
coloured paper
PVA (white) glue
paintbrush
paper fasteners
single hole punch
ribbon

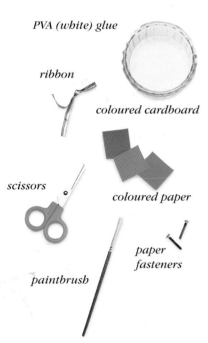

PVA (white) glue

ribbon

coloured cardboard

coloured paper

scissors

paintbrush

paper fasteners

1 Trace the star and circle templates from this book and cut them out with a pair of scissors. Draw round the star template on different coloured pieces of cardboard and cut out the star shapes. Draw round the circle template on pieces of coloured paper and cut out the circles.

2 Cut a piece of cardboard to the size you want your card to be and fold it in half. Glue the paper circles onto the front side of the card.

3 Make a slit in the centre of each star and circle with the scissors. Push a paper fastener through the centre of each star and then push it through one of the circles. Open out the fastener so that it sits flat on the card.

4 Make a gift tag to match the card by using a circle or rectangle of coloured cardboard and paper stars. Punch a hole at one end of the tag and thread a piece of ribbon through it.

Fold-out Greetings Card

Fold-out cards are very versatile – they could simply be decorative like this one, or serve a practical purpose as well. For example, you could cut the words 'Please Come to my Party' from brightly coloured paper and stick them to the third panel to make an unusual and exciting invitation.

YOU WILL NEED
blue medium-weight card
   (posterboard)
pencil
ruler
scissors
thin paper in a variety of colours
non-toxic paper glue

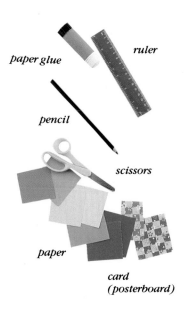

paper glue   *ruler*

pencil

scissors

paper

*card
(posterboard)*

2 Measure a point every 9 cm (3½ in) along the top and bottom of the card. Draw three vertical lines and lightly score along them to make three folds. The first and third lines should be scored on the front of the card and the second on the back.

3 Draw and cut out the pieces of each character from various coloured papers.

1 Draw a rectangle measuring 36 × 20 cm (14 × 8 in) on the card (posterboard). Cut it out.

4 Stick the figures in position on each panel of the card using paper glue.

Woven Paper Cards

Paper weaving is a fun way to achieve exciting effects from a very simple process. Pick your papers with care so that the colours complement each other, or contrast in interesting ways. You can use the weaving as a design on its own, or mount it behind shaped frames to make unusual greetings cards.

YOU WILL NEED
medium-weight card (posterboard) in
  a variety of colours
ruler
pencil
scissors
heavy paper in a variety of colours
non-toxic paper glue

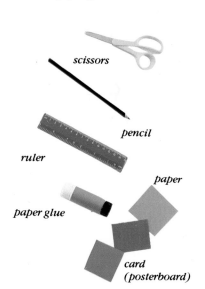

scissors

pencil

ruler

paper

paper glue

card (posterboard)

1 Draw a rectangle measuring 16 × 24 cm (6¼ × 9½ in) on medium-weight green card (posterboard) and cut it out. Draw a line down the centre of the rectangle and gently score along it with scissors to form a fold.

2 Mark a 9 cm (3½ in) square on the front of the card and cut it out to form a window.

3 Cut a piece of red card measuring 10 × 10 cm (4 × 4 in). Make vertical cuts every 1 cm (⅜ in) down the card, from just below the top edge almost to the bottom, but do not cut all the way through.

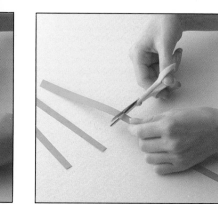

4 Cut several strips of orange paper approximately 1 cm (⅜ in) wide.

5 Weave the orange strips through the red to make a checked pattern. Trim and attach the orange strips at each side of the card with paper glue.

6 Stick the woven square to the inside front of the card so that it shows through the window.

Recycled Paper Greetings Cards

Recycled paper has an appealing, pitted surface that can be very decorative. These cards are collaged from a mixture of different-coloured papers torn from a writing block.

YOU WILL NEED
recycled coloured paper
ruler
pencil
scissors
non-toxic paper glue

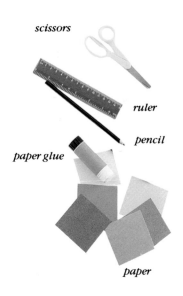

scissors

ruler

pencil

paper glue

paper

1 Take a sheet of recycled paper and draw a rectangle measuring 13 × 26 cm (5¼ × 10¼ in). Cut out the shape and fold it in half to make a card.

4 Using paper glue, stick the square border on the front of the folded card. Stick the heart motif in the middle. You can create additional motifs by tearing designs from coloured paper and sticking them onto cards.

2 Take a sheet of contrasting paper and tear a heart shape out of it.

3 Cut a square of paper in a third colour measuring 12 × 12 cm (4¾ × 4¾ in). Fold it in half. Carefully tear out the middle to leave a ragged border.

Paper Gift Tags

What better way to jazz-up a parcel than these cheerful gift tags? Make them in a variety of colours, wrap your parcels in bright, festive papers and parties will go with a real swing.

YOU WILL NEED
heavy paper in a variety of colours
ruler
pencil
scissors
thin paper in a variety of colours
non-toxic paper glue
hole punch
coloured cord

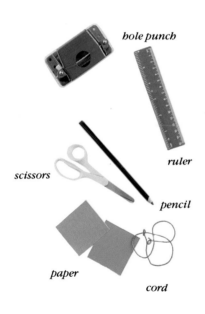

hole punch
ruler
scissors
pencil
paper
cord

1 Draw a rectangle measuring 14 × 8.5 cm (5½ × 3¼ in) on heavy coloured paper and cut it out.

2 Draw an animal head on contrasting thin paper. Cut it out.

3 Divide the rectangle of paper in half. Draw a faint line down the centre of the paper and gently score along the line. Fold the card in half.

4 Stick the animal face to the front of the folded card with paper glue. Make a hole in the top left-hand corner of the back of the card with a hole punch. Tie a loop of cord through the hole.

Birthday Treats

Here is a quick and easy way to make any gift look twice as exciting! The foil or crêpe paper is wrapped around the gift, then a long sheet of cellophane (plastic wrap) is wrapped around to cover it and gathered up at the ends like a giant candy. Twist and tie up with foil ribbon and add a small bag of real wrapped candies instead of a gift tag. A big stack of gifts all wrapped this way would make a wonderful surprise for the birthday person. Use the same idea for small party gifts or prizes.

YOU WILL NEED
bright crêpe paper (foiled or plain)
scissors
sticky tape
ruler
cellophane (plastic wrap), clear
  and coloured
foil ribbon
small bag of wrapped candies
glue

2 Measure the length of your gift and cut the cellophane (plastic wrap) three times that length. Wrap around the gift and secure with tape.

3 Twist the ends and tie them close to the gift, using foil ribbon.

1 Wrap your gift with the coloured crêpe paper, either foiled or plain.

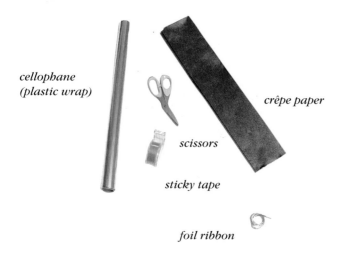

cellophane (plastic wrap)

scissors

crêpe paper

sticky tape

foil ribbon

4 Pull out the cellophane. trimming where necessary, to make a balanced candy shape. Attach a small bag of candies or glue individual wrapped candies to the top of your gift.

Fancy Wrapped Parcels

Turn the humblest present into an exciting parcel by making the wrappings interesting and fun. All sorts of characters are appropriate for decorating parcels. Think of the person who will receive the parcel, and of their favourite characters when choosing a design.

YOU WILL NEED
items to wrap
crêpe paper
sticky tape
paper ribbon
pencil
thin paper in a variety of colours
scissors
non-toxic paper glue
non-toxic strong glue

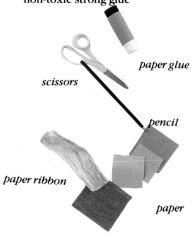

paper glue

scissors

pencil

paper ribbon

paper

crêpe paper

2 Open out lengths of paper ribbon and secure each parcel.

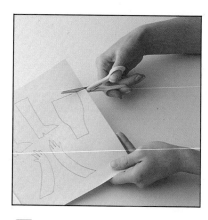

3 Draw designs onto pieces of thin coloured paper to make the head, arms and legs for each parcel (or head, legs and tail if an animal). Cut out the shapes.

1 Wrap the parcels in crêpe paper.

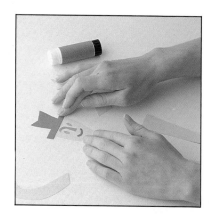

4 Stick the decorative details onto each main body piece with paper glue.

5 Stick the decorations around the corners of each parcel with strong glue.

Origami Gift Wrap

Origami is immensely popular, particularly with children, who enjoy working out and understanding the many complex folding instructions. This gift is wrapped and decorated using the principles of origami. The special folding and tucking means that you do not need to use tape to secure the parcel. The three-dimensional heart shape on the top is a sophisticated decoration that would make an older child feel very grown-up.

YOU WILL NEED
red origami paper
fine, handmade paper
scissors
pencil
PVA (white) glue

PVA (white) glue

scissors

red origami paper

hand-made paper

1 To make the origami heart, take a square of red paper and fold two points across to meet each other on the centre line.

2 Then fold down the top corner to meet the bottom corner. Fold in half again, taking the right edge over to the left edge.

3 Fold the top corners over by 1 cm (½ in) and crease them.

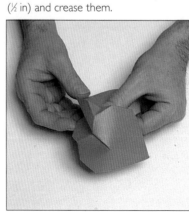

4 Open the shape out – it will have a diamond creased in the middle. Form a valley (inward) fold using the bottom edge of the diamond and extending the fold up to the top edge of the paper.

5 Fold over and tuck in the top two corners. The heart shape appears, raised up in the middle with the point facing downwards.

CRAFT TIP

To achieve sharp paper folds, run the edge of your fingernail along the fold, pressing down firmly.

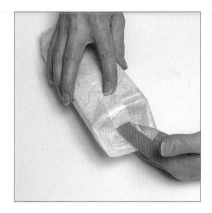

6 To wrap the parcel without tape, fold the top seam over in the usual way then tuck the folded side flap down and in under the gift.

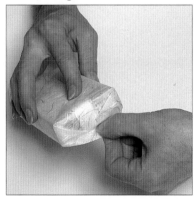

7 Bring the side flaps around, then tuck them with the bottom flap into the same place as the top flap. (Use a blunt instrument, like the round end of a pencil, to tuck all the paper away smoothly.) Position the heart on the gift using PVA (white) glue.

Potato Printing

Create your own wrapping paper with this simple and fun technique.

YOU WILL NEED
potato
knife
felt-tip pen
coloured ink
paper towel
paper plate or saucer for the ink
white or coloured paper

paper

ink

paper towel

knife

potato

paper plate

felt-tip pen

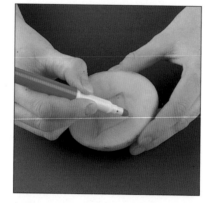

1 Cut a potato in half with a sharp knife and draw out a shape with a felt-tip pen.

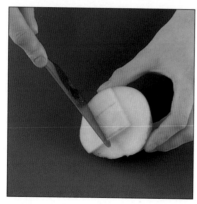

2 Using a sharp knife, cut out the area around the shape.

3 Pour a few drops of ink onto a piece of paper towel placed on a paper plate or saucer and dab the potato into it.

4 Place the potato onto some white or coloured paper and press down hard. Repeat this process until the paper is covered with the design.

Rainforest Wrap

It is impossible to better Nature for shapes, textures and colours – so why try? Leaves make original and stylish gift tags, and look particularly good when teamed with rough hand-made paper and garden raffia. Autumn is the prime time for leaf collecting, but freshly picked leaves can also be used, although the gift should be given on the same day as it is made, to avoid the leaves wilting.

YOU WILL NEED
natural-coloured hand-made paper
scissors
double-sided sticky tape
suitable smooth-surfaced leaves
metallic felt-tip pen
orange raffia

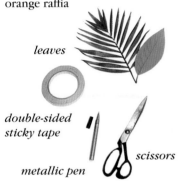

leaves

double-sided sticky tape

metallic pen

scissors

raffia

paper

CRAFT TIP

This present has been given a hot tropical look by the use of palm and avocado pear tree leaves. The leaves are not brittle and can be easily secured with raffia and written on with a metallic felt-tip pen.

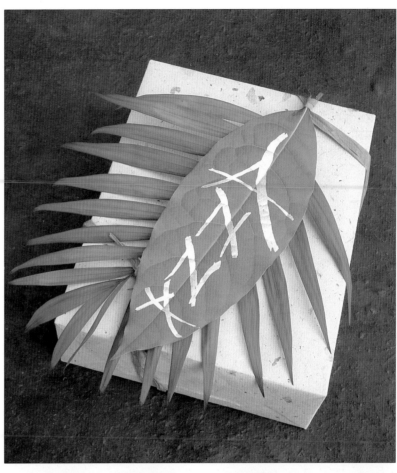

1 Cut the paper to fit your gift.

2 Wrap the present using double-sided tape. Select the leaves, leaving their stalks in place. The leaves should be perfectly shaped, with a smooth surface for writing on.

3 Test the flow of the pen on a piece of scrap paper, then write a name or message on the broadest leaf. Leave to dry for a few minutes.

4 Tie the leaves together, then tie them onto the gift over opposite corners using orange raffia. Trim the raffia ends with scissors.

Edible Labels

If you are making cookies for your party meal, cut out some novel gift labels at the same time. A word of warning – tie them to the gifts at the very last moment, lest the temptation to nibble is too great for the children and the result is a whole pile of unnamed presents!

YOU WILL NEED
ready-mixed cookie dough
rolling pin
board
skewer
cookie cutters
ready-mixed icing
ribbon

cookie cutters

ready-mixed icing

ribbon

*cookie dough mixture
rolling pin
board*

1 Roll out the dough to 1 cm/½ in thick and cut out the cookies using different shaped cutters. Make holes for the ribbon (using a skewer is easiest). Bake in the oven at 180°C/350°F/Gas 4 for 10–12 minutes. Transfer to a wire rack to cool.

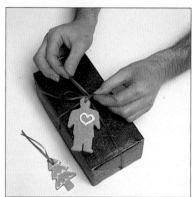

COOK'S TIP
Remember to make a hole in your cookie labels before you bake them.

2 Decorate the cookies by piping on ready-mixed icing.

3 Thread thin ribbon through the holes of the cookie labels.

4 Tie red ribbon around the gift and secure the edible label, so that it lies flat on top of the parcel.

Party Paper Chains

Everyone enjoys making these, and even the youngest children can help with the decorations. If your party has a theme, choose colours and patterns that go with it.

YOU WILL NEED
ruler
cardboard
pencil
scissors
coloured paper
paintbrush
poster paints in various colours
glitter glue
PVA (white)
   glue

glitter glue

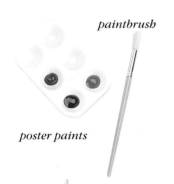
coloured paper

paintbrush

poster paints

scissors

PVA (white) glue

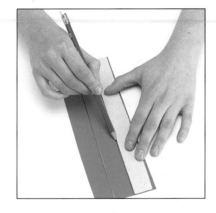

1 Make your own template for the paper chain, as long and as wide as you want. Draw around the template on a piece of coloured paper so that the strips are next to each other. Don't cut the strips out yet.

2 Paint your paper chain strips with lots of bright colours and fun swirls, stripes and dots. Allow the paint to dry.

3 If you like you can add a few dabs of glitter glue to the strips for extra sparkle. Allow the glitter to dry. Cut out all of the decorated strips of paper.

4 Curl the first strip of paper around so that you can glue one end of the strip to the other. Hold it while the glue dries. Thread a second strip of paper through the first loop and glue the ends together. Continue until the chain is really long!

Paper Flowers

Make your own everlasting blooms of colour. You could use them to decorate gift-wrapped presents or to brighten up a room in a colourful container.

YOU WILL NEED
pencil
coloured crêpe paper
scissors
split bamboo canes
green sticky tape
plasticine

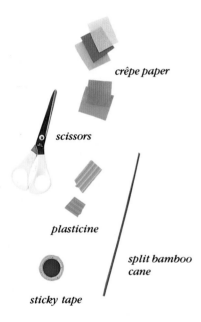

crêpe paper

scissors

plasticine

split bamboo cane

sticky tape

1 With a pencil, draw an assortment of different sized petal shapes onto coloured crêpe paper. Cut them out with a pair of scissors.

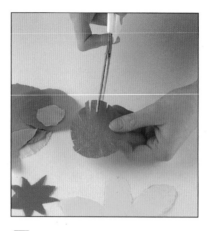

2 Cut around the edge of one of the petal shapes to make a fringe.

3 Starting with the largest petal at the bottom, layer the petals on top of each other, piercing a hole through them with a split bamboo cane.

4 When all the petals are in place, pinch them together and secure with green sticky tape.

5 Roll a piece of plasticine into a ball and place it in the centre of the cane.

6 Fan out the petals to finish off.

Party Brooches

Make a special brooch for each person coming to
the party to wear and keep. Try to give each brooch
a different character, if you like, to suit the person to
whom you are giving it.

YOU WILL NEED
tracing paper
felt-tip pen
scissors
cardboard
poster paints in various colours
paintbrushes
gold paint
wool (yarn)
ribbon
PVA (white) glue
mini pom-pom
star sequins
artificial gemstones
non-toxic strong glue
brooch findings

*poster
paints*

*mini
pom-pom*

scissors

brooch finding

ribbon

paintbrushes

*PVA (white)
glue and
paintbrush*

*wool
(yarn)*

gold paint

*artificial
gemstones*

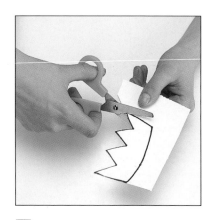

1 Trace all the badge templates from
this book and cut them out. Draw
around the templates on a piece of
cardboard and cut them out.

2 Paint the face-shaped pieces of
cardboard with a flesh colour and paint
the crown shape gold. Allow the paint to
dry completely.

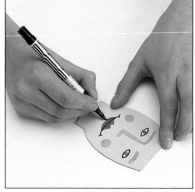

3 Using a fine paintbrush, paint the
eyes, nose and mouth on the faces.
Allow the paint to dry. If you find
painting the details of the face too fiddly,
you could use a felt-tip pen instead.

4 For the girl's hair, cut approximately
nine strands of wool (yarn) to the same
length. Tie them in a knot at the top and
then plait (braid) them. Tie a ribbon at
the end to secure the plait. You will need
two plaits.

5 Glue the end of each plait to the
back of the crown on either side. Allow
the glue to dry. Meanwhile, paint big
stripes on the boy's hat and dots on his
bow tie. When the paint is dry, glue a
mini pom-pom to the tip of his hat.

6 Glue the crown onto the top of the
girl's head. Glue sparkly star sequins onto
the crown and add artificial gemstones
as a necklace. Allow the glue to dry.
Using strong glue stick a brooch finding
onto the back of each and leave the glue
to dry.

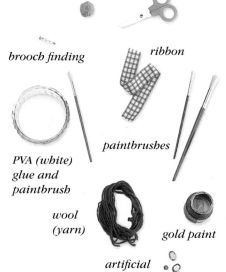

Groovy Party Hats

All your guests will enjoy wearing these wacky hats and they will definitely want to take them home at the end of the party.

YOU WILL NEED
tracing paper
pencil
scissors
thin coloured card (posterboard)
paper fasteners
coloured paper
crêpe paper
ribbon
PVA (white) glue
paintbrush
mini pom-poms or tinsel

coloured cardboard

coloured paper

mini pom-poms

paper fasteners

PVA (white) glue and paintbrush

scissors

ribbon

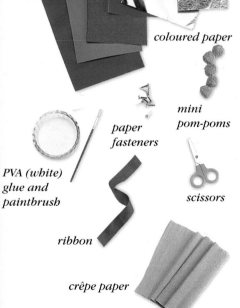

crêpe paper

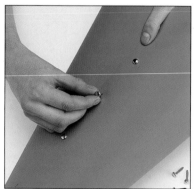

1 Trace the template for the party hat from this book. Scale it up and cut it out. Draw around the template on a large piece of coloured cardboard. Cut out the hat shape and roll it into a cone. Hold the cone shape in place using paper fasteners.

2 Cut out some circles from the coloured paper. You will need circles in two different sizes and a heart shape. Make other fun shapes, such as stars, if you like. Try to make each hat different.

3 Starting with the large circle, place the smaller circle on top and then the heart. Pierce a paper fastener through the shapes. Make a small hole in the hat and push the paper fastener through it.

4 Open out the paper fastener so that it lies flat on the inside of the hat. Roll a piece of crêpe paper into a tight roll and place it in the top of the hat. Using a pair of scissors, snip into the top of the crêpe paper to turn it into a tassel.

5 Measure around the base of the hat and cut a length of ribbon long enough to go around it. Using PVA (white) glue, stick the ribbon carefully around the base of the hat.

6 Glue mini pom-poms or tinsel onto the ribbon around the base of the hat. Allow the glue to dry completely.

COSTUME PARTIES

Children love dressing up and a costume party is a good excuse. Outrageous outfits can be concocted from simple odds and ends, and by adapting and recycling everyday materials such as cardboard and other packaging materials, coloured paper and foil. The kids will enjoy coming up with their own ideas for costumes, perhaps based on their favourite characters, or they can look in this chapter for something fantastic, funny or weird – there are lots of cuddly animals and scary monsters to choose from and other ideas. Face paints are the perfect finishing touch, and you'll find step-by-step instructions to help you achieve some brilliant transformations.

Materials and Equipment

This is a selection of the materials used in this chapter. If you can't find exactly the same materials, see if there is anything else you could substitute.

Baubles (balls)
These can be used to decorate headdresses and other accessories. Only use baubles made from plastic or paper.

Braid
This comes in a range of styles and widths and can be used to decorate clothes and accessories.

Buttons
Interesting buttons can be used as decoration.

Coloured sticky tape
This strong tape can be used for fastening heavy materials. It also can be used for decoration.

Coloured paper
Heavy paper can be used for making hats and headdresses.

Covered elastic cord
This can be purchased from department stores and comes in different colours and strengths. It can be attached to hats to make them easier to wear.

Crêpe and tissue paper
These can be used for decoration. They are quite fragile and are best suited to costumes that will only need to be worn once or twice.

Feathers
These can be bought from sewing shops and can be used to decorate hats and accessories.

Felt
This comes in a range of colours. It is easy to cut and won't fray.

Garden canes
These have many uses. Decorate one and turn it into a fairy's wand, or use several as the stems on a fun bunch of paper flowers.

Glitter
This can be glued on as decoration. If there is any left be sure to pour it back into the tube to use again.

Hairbands
These can be decorated to make a headdress or covered in fur to make a pair of ears.

Hessian (burlap)
This heavy cloth is perfect for costumes. When cut, the cloth may be frayed to make a fringe.

Metal kitchen scourers
These are made of soft metal and are used in the kitchen to clean pots and pans but they also make fun decorations.

Milliner's wire
This is covered with thread and is therefore safer to use than ordinary wire. You should still take care with the sharp ends, and cover them with tape.

Netting
This fabric is perfect for making light, airy skirts and wings. It is available in a wide range of colours from fabric shops.

Newspaper
Save old newspaper and use to protect surfaces when you are working or to make papier mâché.

Paintbrushes
Use a range of different sizes to apply paint and glue.

Paints
Use non-toxic paints to add details. If you don't have exactly the colour you want, try mixing paints together to make new ones.

Poppers (snaps)
These are quicker to add to a costume than buttons and buttonholes.

Ribbons
These come in a range of colours and patterns and can be used for making bows as decoration.

Safety pins
These can be taped onto the back of badges or used to help thread elastic through a waistband.

Sewing thread
Some of the costumes require basic sewing techniques. It is a good idea to match your sewing thread to your main material.

String
String can be used as a single fastener on an outfit, or can be used for hanging pendants.

Supermarket packaging
Boxes, egg cartons, and plastic and foil containers can all be used to make and decorate costumes.

Tin foil
This can be cut up or crumpled to create different decorative effects.

Tinsel
Save spare tinsel from the Christmas tree and use it to create sparkly accessories and details.

Wool
This can be used for making wigs and plaits (braids).

feathers

egg carton

bauble (ball)

metal kitchen scourer

netting

tinsel

braid

crêpe and tissue paper

ribbon

felt

sewing thread

garden canes

foil pie-dish (pan)

string

paper bauble
(ball)

glitter

coloured
sticky tape

newspaper

paints

bessian
(burlap)

tin foil

wool

coloured paper

covered
elastic cord

paintbrushes

hairband

poppers
(snaps)

safety pins

buttons

Face Painting Materials

There is an enormous range of face painting materials available at a range of different prices. Toy and novelty shops often stock a range of face paints, as well as theatrical suppliers.

Child's make-up kit
This is a good starter kit. It includes a bright range of coloured face paints, sponges, brushes, and a well for water. It is available from most toy shops.

Cleansing towels
These are ideal for removing the last traces of face paint.

Cold cream cleanser
Even though most water-based face paints come off with soap and water, you can also use a cream cleanser with soft tissues or cotton wool.

Cotton buds
These are used to apply and remove make-up around the eye.

Eyebrow brush
This is used for combing eyebrows and eyelashes.

Fake blood
This is great for special effects and can be purchased from theatrical and novelty shops.

Glitter gel
This comes in a range of colours and gives a sparkly finish. It can be purchased from costume shops.

Make-up brushes
These come in a range of sizes and shapes. It is a good idea to have different types to use for different effects. Wide brushes either have a flat or rounded edge and are used for large areas of modelling or for applying blusher, highlights or all-over powder. Medium brushes with a rounded edge are useful for modelling colour, while narrow brushes, either flat or pointed, are used for outlining and painting fine details and lips.

Make-up fixative
This is available from professional theatrical shops. It fixes the make-up, therefore making it last longer. Make sure that the model's eyes are closed when spraying it.

Make-up palette
This provides a range of solid, vibrant colours that give very good effects. You can mix colours together if the set you have doesn't provide the range of colours you require.

Make-up (eye-liner) pencils
These are used for drawing fine details on the face. They can also be used for outlining your basic design, if necessary.

Make-up pots
These are purchased from specialist theatrical shops. They are more expensive but are excellent quality and come in a wonderful range of colours.

Plastic palette
Use as a surface for mixing face paints together to achieve more subtle colours.

Soft tissue
Use with a dab of cold cream cleanser to remove make-up or for wiping off excess make-up from your brush.

Sponges
Covered sponges such as powder puffs are used for applying dry powders. Cellulose or latex sponges can be used slightly damp to give an even colour. Stipple sponges are made from soft plastic and are used for creating textured effects such as beard growth, animal skins and other effects.

Temple white
This is available from theatrical shops and is applied to the hair to give an aged effect.

Wax make-up crayons
If you do not mind a less professional finish, these are a good, inexpensive option. They give a less solid colour and the result is less long-lasting but they are often formulated for young children to use themselves.

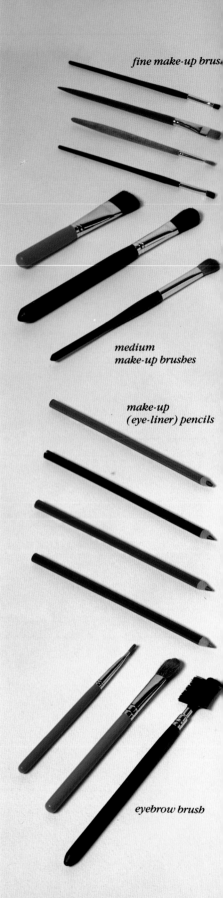

fine make-up brush

medium make-up brushes

make-up (eye-liner) pencils

eyebrow brush

make-up fixative

cleansing towels

child's make-up kit

cold cream cleanser

fake blood

make-up pots

temple white

make-up palette

cotton buds

sponges

plastic palette

soft tissue

wax make-up crayons

glitter gel

wide make-up brushes

Applying a Base

An evenly applied, well-modelled base is the foundation for successful face-painting effects. Experiment with different colours, blended directly onto the face, to change the model's appearance.

YOU WILL NEED
make-up sponge
water-based face paints

1 Using a damp sponge, begin to apply the base colour over the face. To avoid streaks or patchiness, make sure the sponge is not too wet.

2 Make sure the base is applied evenly over the face and fill in any patchy areas.

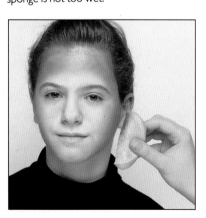

3 Using a contrasting colour, sponge around the edge of the face.

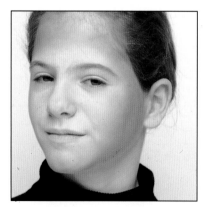

4 Blend the colours together for an even finish. Always make sure the base colours are dry before you start to decorate the face with other colours.

Shading

Shading can change the shape of your model's face dramatically.

YOU WILL NEED
powder face paints
soft make-up brush

1 When shading under the model's eyes, ask her to look up so that the area becomes smooth and easy to work on. This also stops the model from blinking as you work.

2 To exaggerate the shape of the model's face, shade each cheekbone with blusher or dark powder face paint.

3 To shade the whole face, use a large soft brush.

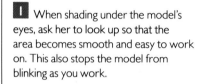

Painting Lips

YOU WILL NEED
fine lipstick brush
water-based face paints

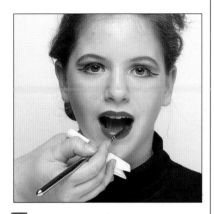

1 Using a fine lipstick brush, paint the lips. Ask the model to close her mouth as this makes the muscles firmer and easier to outline. Then ask the model to open her mouth to fill in the corners. You may need to wait a few seconds to allow the make-up to dry before going on to the next stage.

2 Rest your hand on the model's chin, on a piece of tissue or a powder puff. This will help you to paint an even outline around the lips. You might want to experiment with using a different colour for the outline, or extending the line beyond the natural curve of the model's mouth to create a different shape.

Ageing the Face

You can make even the young look very old with this technique.

YOU WILL NEED
water-based face paints
fine make-up brush
wide make-up brush

1 To find where wrinkles occur naturally, ask the model to frown. This will show where lines will occur with age. Apply fine lines of make-up in these areas. Ask the model to smile, and apply a fine line starting at either side of the nose, down the fold of the cheek.

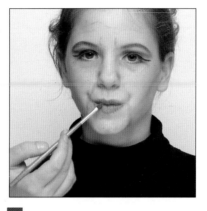

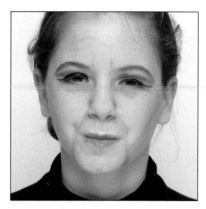

2 Ask your model to purse her lips, and apply fine lines around the mouth, within the natural folds.

3 Finish by giving a light dusting of a lighter coloured base with a wide brush on the cheeks and temples.

Removing Make-up

Most face paints will come off with soap and water. If soap is too drying, or if some colours persist, you may want to remove make-up as follows.

YOU WILL NEED
cold cream cleanser
cotton wool ball or soft tissues

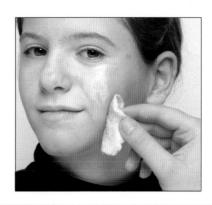

1 Pour the cream onto a damp cotton wool ball or tissue and gently rub the make-up off the face. Use a clean tissue or your fingers to apply more cold cream cleanser.

2 If desired, give a final cleanse with soap and water, and dry by patting the face with a soft towel.

Crowns

These colourful crowns will give your party a regal flavour. Their unusual shape comes from the simple folding and looping of medium-weight paper to very stylish effect.

YOU WILL NEED
medium-weight paper in a variety of
  colours
ruler
pencil
scissors
stapler
sticky tape
non-toxic paper glue

pencil

ruler

scissors

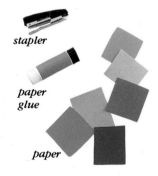

stapler

paper
glue

paper

1 Measure and cut out a large rectangle 19 × 60 cm (7½ × 24 in) from medium-weight paper.

2 Mark a point 7 cm (2¾ in) from the bottom of the rectangle. Draw a central line from side to side. Draw a vertical line from the top of the rectangle to this line every 2 cm (¾ in).

3 Carefully cut down these lines stopping at the lower horizontal line. Cut off the final strip of paper to make a fastening tab.

4 Carefully bring down each strip of paper to form a loop and staple the loops to the remaining strip of paper. Continue all the way around the crown. Bend both ends round to meet and staple and tape the crown at the join.

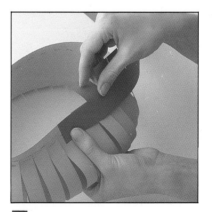

5 Cut a strip of paper 6 × 58 cm (2¼ × 23 in) from paper of a contrasting colour. Draw a central line dividing the strip in half. Make small notches along one edge of the strip up to the central line. Stick this strip around the base of the crown, folding the notched edge to the inside of the crown, to form a band.

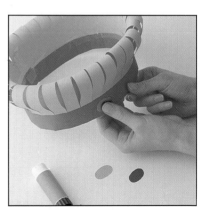

6 Cut ovals of bright paper to represent jewels and stick them around the crown.

Garden Hat

Crown the star of the garden party with this lovely, leafy hat. Add butterflies for extra excitement!

YOU WILL NEED
thin green card (posterboard)
ruler
pencil
scissors
heavy paper in a variety of colours
non-toxic paper glue

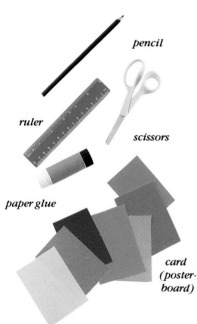

pencil

ruler

scissors

paper glue

card (poster-board)

paper

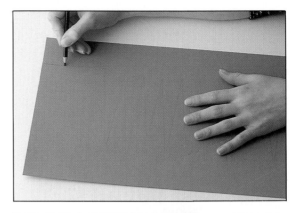

1 Draw a rectangle measuring 22 × 60 cm (8¾ × 24 in) on green card (posterboard). Using the photograph as a guide, mark out the hat on the card. The triangles along the front of the hat should be drawn to varying lengths as they form the stalks of the flowers.

2 Cut out the hat shape, remembering to cut the stalks to different lengths.

3 To make the flowers, cut circles of heavy paper in various bright colours. Snip small pieces of paper from around the edges of each circle to make petal shapes. Decorate each flower with details cut from contrasting paper, and stick in place with paper glue.

4 Cut butterflies from coloured paper and add their markings with scraps of bright paper.

5 Stick the flowers and butterflies around the hat.

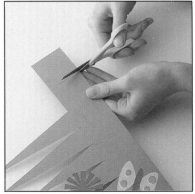

6 Hold the hat around the child's head and mark where the two ends of the hat band meet. Cut a notch in each end of the band to form a fastening.

Making a Tail

This tail was made to go with the spotted dog outfit.
You can make a tail for a cat or tiger in the same way.

YOU WILL NEED
old pair of children's black tights
scissors
newspaper
elastic
needle and thread
felt
fabric glue

newspaper

fabric glue

scissors

tights

1 Cut one leg off the pair of tights. Scrunch up balls of newspaper and fill up the leg until it is quite firm.

2 Tie a knot at the end of the leg.

3 Measure your waist so you know how much elastic you need. Sew the elastic in a loop onto the knotted end of the tail.

4 This tail is for the spotted dog so it has been decorated with spots of felt glued on with fabric glue. You could always paint on a different design using fabric paints.

Making Ears

These ears add a cuddly touch to any of the animal outfits. You can adjust the size of the ears and choose material to suit the animal.

YOU WILL NEED
hairband
tape measure
fake fur
scissors
needle and thread
felt
fabric glue (optional)
template for ears
cardboard
pencil

hairband

scissors

thread

fake fur

1 Measure the length of the hairband with a tape measure. Cut out a piece of fur to fit, allowing an extra 2 cm (1 in) at each end for folding over. Sew the fur on to the hairband as shown.

2 Cut out a piece of felt to fit the inside of the hairband and sew or glue it on.

3 Trace the appropriate template from the back of the book onto a piece of cardboard and draw around the cardboard on the reverse side of the fur. You will need two pieces of fur for each ear. Place the two pieces of fur together with the right sides facing and sew round, leaving a gap to turn the right sides out.

4 Sew the ears onto the hairband, making sure they are in the correct position.

Tiger

For a complete look, you'll need an outfit made from fake tiger fur. Use the instructions earlier in this chapter to make a pair of matching furry ears.

YOU WILL NEED
make-up sponge
water-based face paints
medium make-up brush
fine make-up brush

medium make-up brush

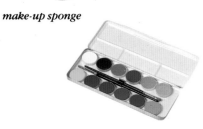

fine make-up brush

make-up sponge

water-based face paints

1 Using a damp sponge, apply the base colour over the face.

2 Rinse the sponge, then stipple a darker shade of paint around the edge of the face as shown.

3 Sponge the chin and the area above the mouth white. Using a medium brush, paint the area around the eyes white as shown. You might find it easier to paint the outline first and then fill it in.

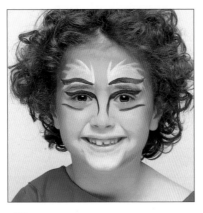

4 Using a medium brush, paint on the black markings around each eye, as shown, making sure each side is the same.

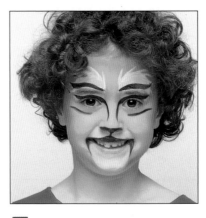

5 Using a fine brush, paint the tip of the nose black and paint a thin black line from the centre of the nose to the top lip. Paint the top lip black and extend the line at each corner of the mouth, stopping half-way down the chin.

6 For the rest of the markings, paint brushstrokes of colour across the face. To keep the design symmetrical, finish one side of the face first and then copy the design onto the other side.

Bumble Bee

A striped outfit to buzz around in. Why not paint a
pair of tights or leggings in the same style?

YOU WILL NEED
yellow T-shirt
newspaper
black fabric paint
paintbrush
paints
hairband
paper baubles (balls)
scissors
milliner's wire
needle and thread
black felt
glue
black cardboard
pencil
needle and thread

FOR THE FACE
make-up sponge
water-based face paints
medium make-up brush

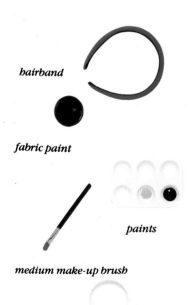

hairband

fabric paint

paints

medium make-up brush

glue

1 Place the T-shirt on a flat, well-
covered surface. Fill the T-shirt with flat
pieces of newspaper. Paint black lines
across the T-shirt and on the arms and
leave the paint to dry. Turn the T-shirt
over to the other side and continue
painting the lines.

4 Fold a piece of black cardboard in
half and draw the shape of a wing, so that,
when it is cut out and the paper is opened
out, you will have two identical wings that
are joined together. Sew the wings along
the fold onto the back of the T-shirt.

2 For the antennae, first paint the
hairband black and leave the paint to dry.
Paint the paper baubles (balls) yellow and,
when the paint has dried, paint a black line
around each one.

3 Cut a length of wire, approximately
45 cm (18 in) long. Bend the wire to fit
the hairband, making sure each piece of
wire that will support the bauble is the
same length. Sew the wire on to the
hairband and glue a strip of black felt
over the wire for extra support. Secure
the baubles on to the ends of the wire.

5 For the face, use a damp sponge to apply a yellow base. Using a medium brush, paint
a black line on the eyelids and under each eye. Paint a black spot on the tip of the nose.

Spotted Dog

This funny dog's outfit is easy to make. Simply cut out circles of felt and stick them onto a pair of leggings and a T-shirt using fabric glue. Use the template and the instructions provided earlier to make a pair of spotted ears and a tail to match.

YOU WILL NEED
make-up sponge
water-based face paints
fine make-up brush
medium make-up brush

make-up sponge

water-based face paints

fine make-up brush

medium make-up brush

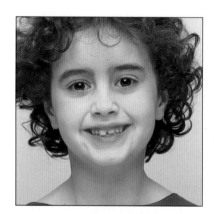

1 Using a damp sponge, apply a white base colour over the face. Gently sponge a slightly darker shade around the eyes.

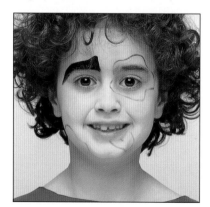

2 Paint one eyebrow black and, using a fine make-up brush, paint a wiggly outline around the other eye to make a patch. Paint another patch outline on the side of the face. Paint the outline for a droopy tongue below the bottom lip.

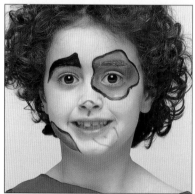

3 Using a medium brush fill in the patches grey and outline them in black. Draw the outline for the nose and a line joining the nose to the mouth.

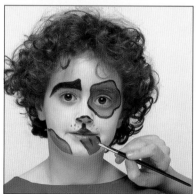

4 Fill in the tongue red and outline in black. Paint a short black line along the centre of the tongue. Fill in the tip of the nose pink and add a thick black line where the nose joins the mouth. Paint the centre of the top lip black. Paint black whisker spots under the nose.

Panda

If you only have a few face paints, this is the perfect project for you. It is good for beginners as it is simple to do. Use the template and the instructions provided earlier to make a pair of furry ears to match.

YOU WILL NEED
black make-up (eye-liner) pencil
make-up sponge
water-based face paints
medium make-up brush
fine make-up brush

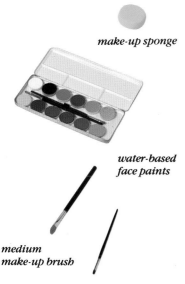

make-up sponge

water-based face paints

medium make-up brush

fine make-up brush

1 Using a black make-up (eye-liner) pencil, gently draw an outline around each eye as shown. Draw an outline across the tip of the nose.

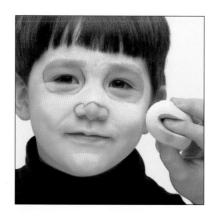

2 Using a damp sponge, apply a white base over the face, avoiding the areas you have just marked with the pencil.

3 Using a medium brush, paint the eyes and the tip of the nose black. Using a fine brush, paint a line joining the nose to the mouth and paint the lips. Paint small whisker spots either side of the mouth. Add black lines between the eyebrows.

Witch

This young witch looks like she's got a few tricks up her sleeve. She is wearing a cloak made from an old piece of fabric and long black nails.

YOU WILL NEED
tape measure
black fabric for hat
iron-on interfacing (optional)
pencil
scissors
needle and thread
raffia or straw

FOR THE FACE
make-up sponge
water-based face paints
lipstick brush
fine make-up brush
thick make-up brush

1 To make the hat, measure around the head so that you know how wide to make the rim of the hat. If the fabric you are using needs to be stiffened, iron a piece of interfacing on to the reverse side. Draw and cut out a triangle with a curved base, making sure the rim measures the circumference of the head with a small allowance for sewing the fabric together.

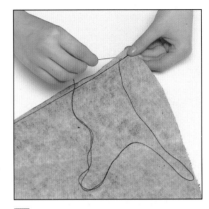

2 With the right sides facing, fold the triangle in half to form a tall cone and sew along the side.

3 Make bundles of raffia or straw and tie a knot in the centre of each bundle. Sew each bundle around the rim of the hat leaving a gap at the front. The more bundles you sew on, the wilder the wig will be. Turn the hat the right way out.

black fabric

thread

raffia

iron-on interfacing

4 For the face, use a damp sponge to dab the base colours over the face.

5 Using a lipstick brush, paint on a pair of wild, black eyebrows. Paint a black line on each eyelid just above the eyelashes. Paint a line of red just under each eye and a black curve below it.

6 Add ageing lines with a fine brush Build more colour onto the cheeks using a thick make-up brush. Paint the lips red, exaggerating the top lip.

scissors

Ghost

This simple outfit makes a fabulous disguise. See how long it takes everyone to guess who is underneath.

YOU WILL NEED
old white sheet
scissors
needle and thread or sewing machine
milliner's wire
black felt
fabric glue

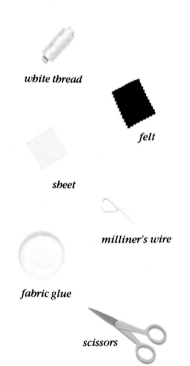

white thread

felt

sheet

milliner's wire

fabric glue

scissors

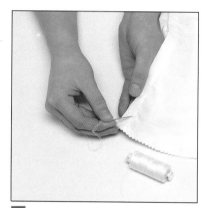

1 Cut two pieces of sheet in the shape of a dome, making sure the height of the dome is longer than the child's height. Sew the two pieces together leaving an opening at the bottom. Sew another line of stitching parallel to the line you have sewn. This is to make a tube for the wire.

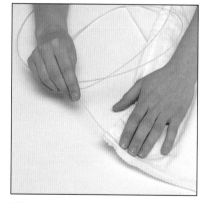

2 Thread the wire through the tube. Secure each end of the wire to the sheet with a few stitches.

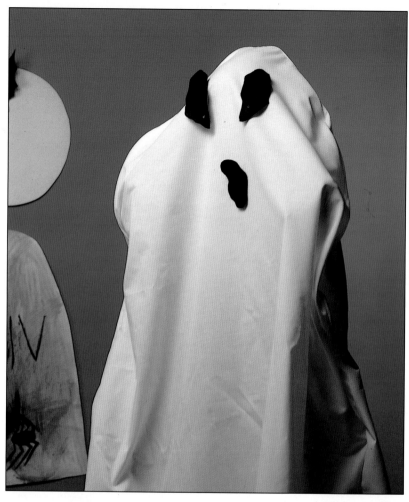

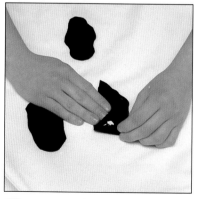

3 Cut out a mouth and pair of eyes from a piece of felt and glue them onto the sheet using fabric glue.

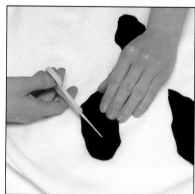

4 Cut small holes in the eyes and the mouth, so that you can see where you are going. Try the costume on and bend the wire to fit the body.

Egyptian Mummy

Make sure there is a white T-shirt and a pair of white tights or leggings underneath the costume, just in case it starts to unravel!

YOU WILL NEED
old white sheet
scissors
needle and thread
white T-shirt and leggings or tights

FOR THE FACE
make-up sponge
water-based face paints

sheet

thread

scissors

water-based face paints

make-up sponge

1 To make the costume, tear or cut strips of the sheet approximately 10 cm (4 in) wide and as long as possible.

2 Sew the strips of fabric together to form one long strip.

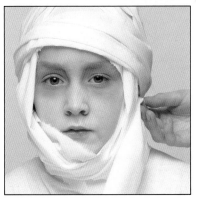

3 For the face, use a damp sponge to apply a white base. Rinse the sponge, then dab light purple around the eye sockets to give a ghoulish appearance. Then wrap the fabric round the head first, leaving the face open. Gradually wrap the fabric down the body.

4 When you get to the hands, go back up the arm again, still wrapping the fabric around. Do the same with the legs. When you have wrapped the whole body, sew the end of the strip to part of the costume. To take the costume off, simply unravel the strip of fabric.

Vampire

This haunted face will scare everyone at the party.
You'll need an all-black costume to set it off.

YOU WILL NEED
make-up sponge
water-based face paints
medium make-up brush
fine make-up brush
black make-up (eyeliner) pencil
   (optional)
red make-up (eyeliner) pencil
fake blood (optional)

water-based face paints

fake blood

fine make-up brush

medium make-up brush

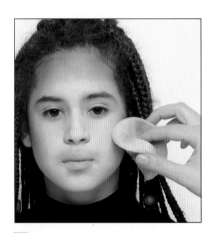

1 Using a damp sponge, apply a base colour on the face. Rinse the sponge, then dab a slightly darker shade on the forehead, blending it with the base colour.

2 Using a medium brush, paint a triangle in the centre of the forehead, one on either side of the face at the cheekbones and a small one at the bottom of the chin. You might find it easier to draw the outline for each shape first, to make sure they are symmetrical, and then fill them in.

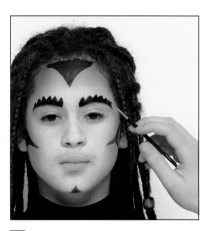

3 Using a fine brush paint a pair of jagged eyebrows over the model's own. Again, you may find it easier to draw the outline first.

4 Paint the eyelids white and the area up to the eyebrows grey. Use the red make-up pencil to colour the area under the eyes .

5 Exaggerate the points on the top lip and colour the lips black.

6 Paint the outline of long, pointed fangs under the bottom lip and fill them in with yellow. Dab fake blood or red make-up at the points of the fangs and at the corners of the eyes.

Dinosaur

Dress up your own prehistoric monster in this spiky camouflaged outfit.

YOU WILL NEED
green fabric or felt
scissors
green polo neck (turtleneck) or
T-shirt
fabric glue
needle and thread
fire resistant stuffing (batting)
hairband
green paint
paintbrush
glue

FOR THE FACE
make-up sponge
water-based face paints
stipple sponge
medium make-up brush

hairband

thread

fabric

fabric glue

stuffing (batting)

scissors

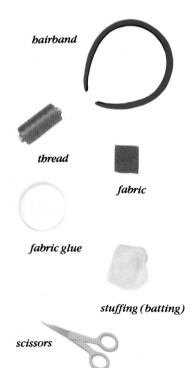

1 To make the costume, cut out lots of triangles, more or less the same size, from a piece of old green fabric or felt. You could use different coloured green fabrics if you don't have enough of one kind.

2 Starting at the bottom of the shirt, glue on the fabric spikes so that they overlap each other. Leave a circle in the centre of the shirt empty.

3 For each spike on the spine, you will need to cut out two triangles. Sew the two triangles together with right sides facing. Turn the triangles right side out and fill with stuffing (batting) to make a spike shape. Sew a running stitch around the bottom edge of the spike and pull gently. This will draw up the threads and close the spike. Tie a knot.

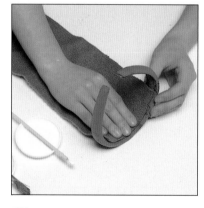

4 Paint the hairband green and leave it to dry. Cut a strip of green fabric approximately 10 cm (4 in) wide and however long you wish it to be. Using glue, secure the strip onto the inside of the hairband and leave to dry.

5 Sew the spikes onto the strip of fabric attached to the hairband.

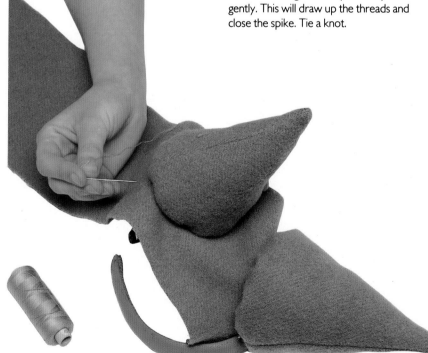

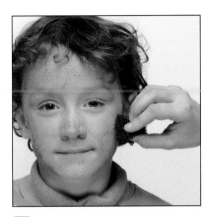

6 For the face, use a damp sponge to apply the base colour over the face. Using a stipple sponge, dab a darker shade over the base colour.

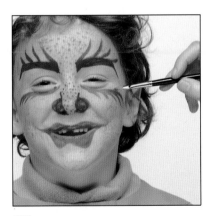

7 Using a medium brush, decorate the face. Paint on wild eyebrows, exaggerated nostrils, spots, big lips and markings under each eye.

Ballerina

This pretty tutu is great for showing off ballet steps. Make it the same colour as a ballet leotard.

<small>YOU WILL NEED</small>
2 metres/2 yards coloured netting
needle, thread and pins
tape measure
wide ribbon for the waistband
narrow ribbon for the bows
scissors
matching leotard and tights

narrow ribbon

thread

netting

wide ribbon

scissors

1 Fold the netting over lengthwise and sew a line of running stitch along the folded edge. Measure your ballerina's waist. For a short tutu, fold over again, and secure with running stitches. Pull the thread gently to gather the netting to fit the waist and tie a knot or sew a few stitches to secure the gathers.

2 Pin the wide ribbon onto the gathered netting and then sew it on.

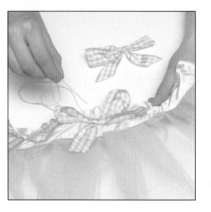

3 Using the narrower ribbon, tie approximately six small bows. Sew five bows onto the waistband.

4 To finish the costume, sew the last bow onto the leotard.

Fairy

This sparkling outfit could make a special wish come true. To complete the effect, add a white leotard and pin some tinsel in the hair.

YOU WILL NEED
2 metres/2 yards netting
needle and thread
scissors
tinsel
1.5 metres/1½ yards white fabric
milliner's wire
silver elastic cord
garden cane
silver paint
paintbrush
silver paper or cardboard
sticky tape
glue
white leotard and tights

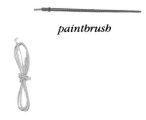
paintbrush

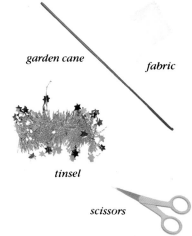
milliner's wire

garden cane

fabric

tinsel

scissors

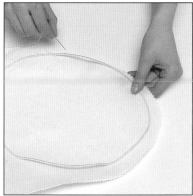

1 To make the tutu, follow the instructions for the ballerina tutu, folding the netting lengthwise once only for a longer skirt. Instead of decorating the waistband with ribbon, sew on a piece of tinsel. Cut out two pieces of white fabric for the wings, in a figure-of-eight shape. On the wrong side of one of the pieces of fabric, sew a separate length of wire around each wing.

2 Place the other piece of fabric on top of the first, making sure the wrong sides are facing. Sew around the edge to secure the two pieces together.

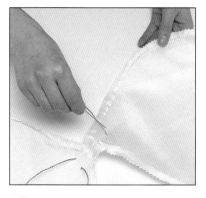

3 Sew a loop of elastic cord onto each wing, near the centre. These will slip over the arms to support the wings on the body.

4 To make the wand, first paint a garden cane silver and leave it to dry. Cut out two silver stars and fasten the silver stick on to the reverse side of one of the stars with a piece of sticky tape. Glue the stars together.

Scarecrow

If you don't have any suitable old clothes of your own, visit a second-hand clothes shop or rummage through piles of clothes at a local flea market. The older the clothes are the better the costume will be.

YOU WILL NEED
raffia
old felt hat
scissors
plastic toy mouse
glue
needle and thread
old clothes, such as a jacket and
    trousers (pants)
scraps of fabric
orange cardboard
orange paint
paintbrush
elastic cord

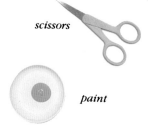

fabric

cardboard

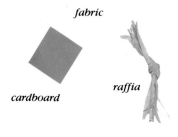

raffia

scissors

paint

1 Tie a few strands of raffia around the hat. Cut a fringe into the rim of the hat with a pair of scissors. Glue a plastic mouse on the top of the hat.

2 Tie bundles of raffia in a knot and sew the bundles around the inside rim of the hat, leaving a gap at the front.

3 Cut ragged edges on the jacket and the trousers (pants).

4 Cut scraps of fabric into squares and rectangles and sew them onto the jacket and the trousers.

5 To make the nose, cut a piece of orange cardboard into a cone shape. Roll the cardboard into a cone and glue it together.

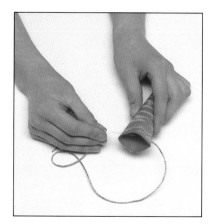

6 Paint orange lines around the cone and leave them to dry. Make a small hole on either side of the cone and thread a piece of elastic cord through that will fit around the head. Tie a knot at each end of the elastic.

Robot

The fun part of this project is collecting all the bits and pieces to recycle. Ask your friends and family to help you collect interesting boxes, cartons and packages.

YOU WILL NEED
2 cardboard boxes
pencil
scissors
silver spray paint
cartons and containers made of
  cardboard and clear plastic
glue
3 Christmas baubles (balls)
foil pie-dishes (pans)
masking tape
pair of old shoes
2 metal kitchen scourers
silver or grey tights
tin foil

foil pie-dish
(pan)

Christmas
bauble (ball)

metal kitchen
scourer

egg carton

glue

silver spray

scissors

1 To make the helmet you will need a cardboard box that fits comfortably over the child's head. Draw a square on one side of the box and cut it out.

2 Spray the box silver. You should do this outdoors or in a very airy room where the surfaces are well covered and protected. When the paint has dried, glue a clear plastic carton over the square hole. Punch a few holes in the cartonto let air through.

3 Decorate the box by gluing on Christmas baubles (balls) and foil pie-dishes (pans).

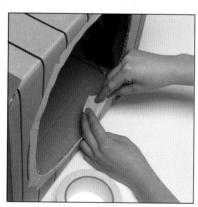

4 For the body of the robot, you will need a large cardboard box. Draw and cut out a hole on the top of the box for the head and one on either side for the arms. Secure the edges of the holes with masking tape.

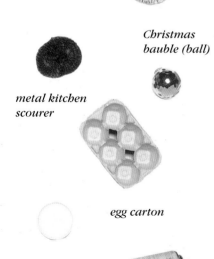

5 Decorate the robot body by gluing on all the boxes and containers you have been collecting. When the glue has dried, spray the box silver, following the same instructions as in step 2. Leave the paint to dry thoroughly before trying the costume on the child.

6 Spray a pair of old shoes silver and decorate them with metal kitchen scourers or anything shiny. Finally, once the costume is on, wrap the child's arms in tin foil.

Knight

This shiny suit of armour is perfect for pretend battles and other daring adventures.

YOU WILL NEED
cardboard
scissors
tin foil
black felt
glue
coloured foil paper
template for helmet
pencil
silver paint
paintbrush
template for body shield
hole puncher
ribbon

paint

glue

scissors

coloured foil paper

tin foil

1 Cut a piece of cardboard in the shape of a sword. Cover the blade in silver foil. Cut two pieces of felt to fit the handle of the sword and glue them on. Decorate the handle with diamond shapes cut out of foil paper.

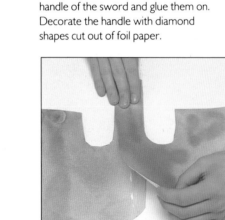

2 To make the helmet, use the template to draw and cut two equal pieces of cardboard. Paint these silver and leave to dry. Glue the two pieces together as shown in the picture.

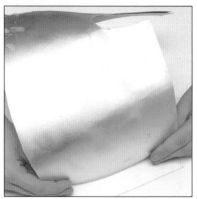

3 When the glue has dried, fold the helmet so that it curves and glue the sides together. Hold the helmet together while the glue dries. To make the body shield you will need to draw round the shape, then flip it to complete the other half. Do this for the front and back pieces and cut them out.

4 Paint the two pieces silver. When the paint has dried, glue the two pieces together at the shoulder seam. Cut a foil paper cross and glue it onto the front of the shield. Punch a hole on either side of the body shield and thread a piece of ribbon through. Tie a knot to secure.

Native American

You can buy the feathers for this costume from most good fabric shops. You can make the skirt from felt with an elastic waistband.

YOU WILL NEED
tape measure
wide ribbon
scissors
feathers
felt
fabric glue
needle and embroidery threads
wool
narrow ribbon

FOR THE FACE
water-based face paints
medium make-up brush

feather

thread

felt

fabric glue

scissors

ribbon

1 Measure around the head with a tape measure, allowing a 5 cm (2 in) overlap and cut the wide ribbon to this length. Arrange the feathers in the centre of the ribbon on the reverse side. Cut a strip of felt the same width as the ribbon and glue it on to the feathers. This will help to secure them in place.

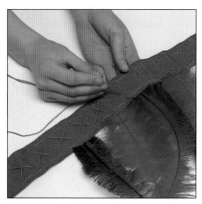

2 Sew a few lines of decorative stitching along the ribbon, using colourful embroidery threads. With the right sides facing, sew the two ends of the ribbon together.

3 To make each plait (braid), you will need approximately 45 equal strands of wool. Tie a piece of wool around one end of each bundle. Ask a friend to help you with the plaiting by holding one end of the bundle tight while you plait. Tie a piece of ribbon in a bow at the end of each plait.

4 Sew or glue the plaits on to the inside of the headdress, so that they lie on either side of the face. For the face, use bright colours to paint three zig-zag lines on each cheek.

Prince

To make a sword, follow the instructions given for the knight's costume. The cloak was made from a piece of fabric found at a flea market and was decorated with a piece of tinsel to match the crown.

YOU WILL NEED
tape measure
pencil
scissors
cardboard
silver paint
paintbrush
coloured foil paper
glue
glitter
tinsel
fabric for cloak
safety pins

coloured foil paper

scissors

glitter

glue

tinsel

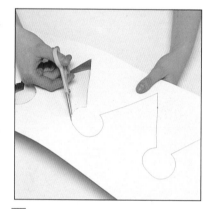

1 Measure around the head with a tape measure so that you know approximately how big to make the crown. Draw and cut out the crown from a piece of cardboard.

2 Paint the cardboard silver and leave the paint to dry thoroughly. Cut shapes out of coloured foil paper and glue them onto the crown. Paint dots of glue onto the shapes and sprinkle on some glitter.

3 Glue a piece of tinsel around the rim of the crown and leave the glue to dry.

4 Glue the two ends of the crown together so that it fits and leave the glue to dry before trying the crown on. Pin the fabric to the child's shoulders to make a cloak.

Princess

Turn a flowing nightdress or party dress into a costume for a fairytale princess by adding this lovely tall headdress with its dreamy veil.

YOU WILL NEED
tape measure
fabric for hat
fabric interfacing (optional)
pencil
scissors
needle and thread
chiffon fabric
wool
narrow ribbon
braid

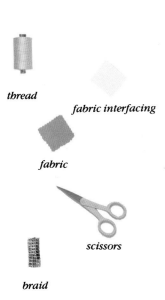

thread

fabric interfacing

fabric

scissors

braid

I Measure the child's head with a tape measure, so that you know how wide to make the rim of the hat. If the fabric you are using needs to be stiffened, iron a piece of interfacing onto the reverse side. Draw and cut out a triangle with a curved base, making sure the rim matches the size of the head, plus an allowance for sewing together. Sew a hem around the rim of the triangle and, with the right sides facing, fold the triangle in half, trapping a piece of chiffon fabric at the point of the cone.

2 Sew the cone together and turn it right side out.

3 Following the instructions for the Native American, make a pair of woollen plaits (braids) and tie a piece of ribbon in a bow around the end of each one. Sew the plaits onto the inside of the hat, so that they lie either side of the face.

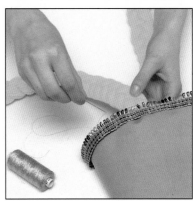

4 Sew a piece of braid around the rim of the hat, and arrange the chiffon fabric so that it trails down the side like a veil.

Super Hero

The perfect outfit for the hero of the day.

YOU WILL NEED
cardboard
scissors
tin foil
coloured foil paper
glue
silver cardboard
ribbon
sticky tape
leotard or catsuit
2 metres (2 yards) fabric
needle and thread

silver cardboard

coloured foil papers

scissors

glue

1 To make a wristband, first cut out a cardboard triangle and cover it in tin foil. Cut a smaller triangle in coloured foil paper and glue it onto the silver triangle. Cut out the letter "S" in silver cardboard and glue it onto the coloured triangle. Cut a strip of silver cardboard 5 cm (2 in) wide and long enough to fit around the wrist. Glue the two ends together to make a band and glue on the triangle. Make another wristband the same way.

2 To make the waistband, cut a piece of cardboard to fit around the waist. Cut a circle from cardboard and cover it in tin foil. Cut a star from coloured foil paper and glue it onto the silver circle. Cut out the letter "S" in cardboard and glue it onto the star.

3 Glue the circle onto the waistband. At each end of the waistband, attach a piece of ribbon with sticky tape. To make the headband, cut a strip of silver cardboard to fit around the head.

4 Cut a circle in coloured foil paper. Cut a smaller circle in a different colour and glue it to the centre of the large circle. Cut out a silver letter "S" and glue it on the circles. Cut a smaller "S" in coloured foil paper and glue it onto the silver "S". Make a cape as opposite.

Super Heroine

Invest the party person with heroic powers by dressing her up in this futuristic costume.

YOU WILL NEED
cardboard
scissors
tin foil
coloured foil paper
glue
silver cardboard
ribbon
sticky tape
coloured cardboard (optional)
leotard or catsuit
2 metres/2 yards fabric
needle and thread

scissors

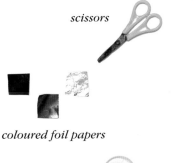

coloured foil papers

glue

1 Make the wristband, waistband and headband as for the Super Hero's outfit.

2 To make the pendant, cut out a star in silver or coloured cardboard and glue the letter "S" onto it. On the back of the star, attach a piece of ribbon in a loop with strong sticky tape.

3 To make the costume you will need a leotard or catsuit. Sew one end of the fabric onto the leotard shoulder straps to make the cloak.

4 Where the fabric joins the straps, glue on silver cardboard triangles.

PARTY FUN AND GAMES

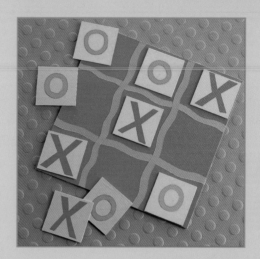

As well as traditional games, which are always a success at kids' parties, you can vary the pace with different kinds of fun. When your guests start to arrive, it's a good idea to break the ice with an activity like making their own party hats or masks, or decorating bags to take their goodies home in. They'll chat and relax while they're absorbed in this, and the later arrivals can just join in whenever they are ready.

They could make some puppets and then stage a show, or have a concert with some home-made musical instruments. From original board games to magic tricks, you'll find ideas here to make your party a sure-fire success.

Materials and Equipment

Coloured pencils and crayons
These must be non-toxic. They come in a huge variety of colours and are useful for decorating projects.

Cotton string
Cotton string comes in a variety of colours and is useful for binding pages together, stringing beads and making picture hangers.

Eye pins
These are small metal pins with a loop at one end. They are used mostly in jewellery to join items such as earrings together. They can be bought from specialist craft and hobby shops.

Hole punch
Use with adult supervision to make holes in paper for decoration or practical purposes.

Household sponge
This can be cut into small squares and used to apply paint with or without stencils.

Ink pad
Use an ink pad with non-toxic ink to stamp stationery and other projects.

Masking tape
Masking tape is cream-coloured paper tape that can be removed once it has been stuck down. It is particularly useful for keeping joints in position whilst glue dries.

Paintbrushes
Paintbrushes in a variety of thicknesses are used for applying glue and paint.

Paints
These must be non-toxic. Use bright, fast-drying poster paints for your party games and activities.

Paper clips
Paper clips are very useful for holding small pieces of paper together while you are working on a project.

Paper fasteners
These are split metal pins that open out to hold pieces of paper together. They should only be used under adult supervision.

Paper glue
This must be non-toxic. Paper glue comes in a variety of formats. Perhaps the easiest to use is the solid stick of glue.

PVA (white) glue
This must be non-toxic.

Undiluted PVA glue is very useful for sticking heavy cardboard. Diluted, it can be used for papier-mâché.

Rubber cutting mat
These mats are non-slip and protect work surfaces when cutting paper and card.

Ruler
Use for measuring and drawing straight lines.

Scissors
These should be of the type made specially for children with rounded blades.

Sequins
Sequins in various shapes and sizes make very good decorations.

Stapler and staples
These should be used under adult supervision. Staples are very useful for holding paper together, especially joints in fairly thick papers and cards.

Sticky tape
Clear sticky tape is good for sticking paper, cord and card.

Strong glue
This must be non-toxic and solvent-free. Strong glue is sometimes used to fix heavyweight papers.

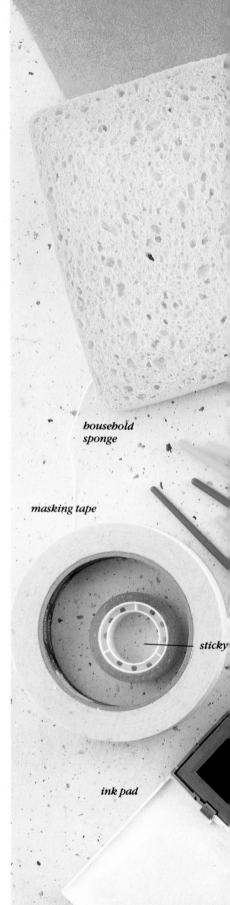

household sponge

masking tape

sticky

ink pad

coloured
pencils

rubber
cutting
mat

cotton string

paper clips

crayons

eye pins

strong glue

eraser

darning elastic

ruler

sequins

stapler

scissors

pencil sharpener

sequins

staples

paper glue

paintbrushes

paper fasteners

hole punch

paints

PVA (white) glue

Eye Masks

Even if you are not holding a masked ball, these disguises are fun to make and wear. You could make one for each guest before the party–or it would be even more fun to get everyone to decorate their own mask when they arrive.

YOU WILL NEED
tracing paper or graph paper
pencil
thin card (posterboard) in a variety of
    colours
scissors
paper in a variety of colours
non-toxic paper glue
thin wooden sticks
paintbrush
non-toxic paint
non-toxic strong glue
wax crayons
gold paper

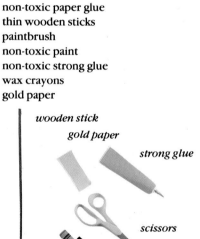

wooden stick
gold paper
strong glue
scissors
crayons
pencil
paper glue
paper
tracing paper
paint

1 Trace or scale up the fiery mask shape from the template at the back of the book and transfer to orange card (posterboard). Cut it out.

2 Place the card on purple paper. Extend the sides and top of the eye mask with small spikes. Cut out this shape.

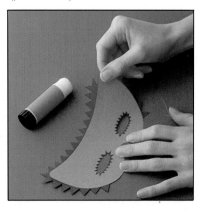

3 Using paper glue stick the orange shape in place on top of the purple one. Carefully trim the lower edge of the mask if necessary.

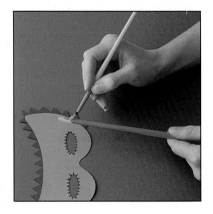

4 Paint the wooden stick a bright colour. You may have to use two coats of paint.

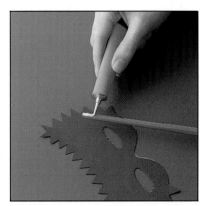

5 Attach the wooden stick to the side of the mask with strong glue. Stick it the right of the mask if you are right-handed and vice-versa if you are left-handed.

6 To make the leopard mask, use yellow card and apply the spots with wax crayon. The king has a crown made of gold paper, and his eyebrows are applied with wax crayon.

Paper-bag Animal Masks

Plain paper bags are great for making masks quickly and easily. You can cut them into all sorts of different shapes and use felt-tipped pens to add exciting decoration. The party guests can transform themselves into their favourite animals, then everyone can go wild in the garden.

YOU WILL NEED
pencil
large paper bags
scissors
paper glue
felt-tip pens

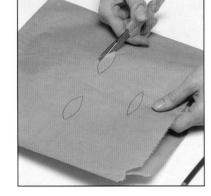

felt-tip pens

paper bag

pencil

scissors

glue

1 Draw three holes on the front of a paper bag, for the eyes and mouth. Cut out the holes.

2 Draw two ears along the top edge of the bag and cut them out. Glue the top edges of the bag together again.

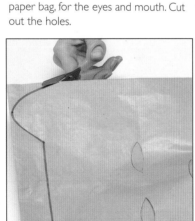

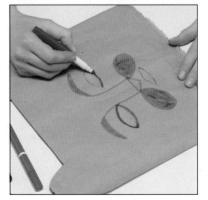

3 Draw the animal's face on the front of the bag, using felt-tip pens. Draw red lines around the eyes so that they stand out strongly.

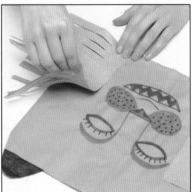

4 To make the lion's mane, cut three wide strips from another paper bag. Make long cuts along one long edge of each strip. Glue the uncut edges of the strips to the sides and top of the head.

90

Blow Painting

You will be amazed at the beautiful colours and wonderful shapes you can create by using this very simple technique.

YOU WILL NEED
coloured paints
water
plastic cups
paper
straws

plastic cup

paper

straws

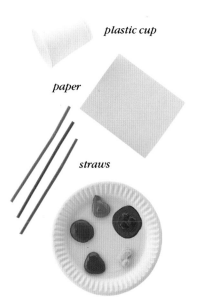

paints

1 Mix each different colour of paint together with water in separate plastic cups.

2 Pour drops of the different-coloured paint mixtures onto a piece of paper.

3 Using a straw, blow the paint around the paper to make a pattern.

4 Add more drops of the paint mixture onto the paper and continue blowing until you are happy with the pattern you have made.

Snake Sock-puppets

One good way to give odd socks a new lease of life is to make them into puppets, using scraps of brightly coloured felt to decorate them. You can make other animals as well as snakes, cutting ears and manes from felt, then have a puppet show.

YOU WILL NEED
coloured felt scraps
scissors
PVA (white) glue
socks

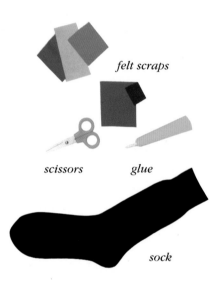

felt scraps

scissors *glue*

sock

1 To make the snake's eyes, cut two circles of felt. Cut two smaller circles of a different colour and glue them to the middle of the larger circles.

2 Glue the snake's eyes in position at the top of the sock.

3 Cut diamonds and strips of felt in various colours. Glue the strips at equal distances along the length of the sock. Glue the diamonds between the strips.

4 Cut a forked tongue from red felt. Glue the tongue to the top of the toe of the sock, in the centre. Allow the glue to dry thoroughly before you play with your sock puppets.

Finger Puppets

Finger puppets are quick and easy to make, and are especially good for entertaining young children. If you decide to make familiar characters from books, you can perform short plays to accompany traditional fairy stories and folk tales.

YOU WILL NEED
tracing paper
pencil
medium-weight coloured paper in a
    variety of colours
scissors
non-toxic paper glue

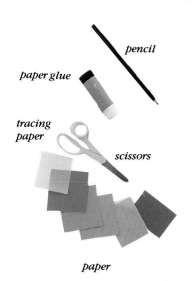

pencil

paper glue

tracing paper

scissors

paper

1 Trace the pig and wolf shapes from the templates. Transfer the wolf to orange paper and the pig three times to pink. Cut out each animal.

2 Cut eyes and noses for each animal from small scraps of coloured paper and stick them in place with paper glue.

3 Cut a small strip of paper approximately 2 cm (¾ in) wide and long enough to fit around your fingers for each puppet. Stick each animal in the centre of a strip.

4 Stick the ends of each finger band together. Allow the puppets to dry thoroughly before playing with them.

Modelling Balloon Dog

Modelling balloons are great fun at parties; buy a big bag and let everyone have a go. Don't worry if your first attempt looks more like a bunch of grapes than a dog – keep trying! Remember, the size of your dog depends on how much you have inflated the balloon. Your model could look like anything from a sausage dog to a poodle!

YOU WILL NEED
modelling balloon
balloon pump

modelling balloon

balloon pump

1 Inflate the balloon, leaving 10 cm (4 in) uninflated at the end. Now twist three bubbles 6–8 cm (2¼–3½ in) in length and keep hold of them.

CRAFT TIP

Once you've made your first model, try making more with different-sized ears, bodies and legs. It's good practice for later models and you may end up inventing an animal of your own.

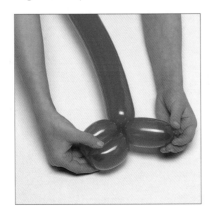

2 To form the ears, twist the second and third bubbles together. They should now be locked in place, even when you let go. This is the dog's head.

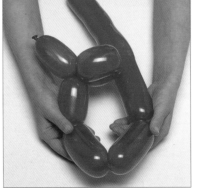

3 The front legs are made by twisting two slightly larger bubbles together and locking them in position. Remember to leave a gap for the animal's neck.

4 Finally, leave a portion of balloon for the body and twist together two bubbles to make the back legs. The very end of the balloon forms the tail.

Modelling Balloon Swan

Here's another simple design to try making at your party: if you have a pool in the garden (yard), you can see how well these swans swim.

YOU WILL NEED
modelling balloon
balloon pump

modelling balloon

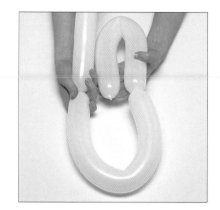

1 Inflate the balloon, leaving only a very short uninflated end. Make two large bubbles in the balloon about 35 cm (14 in) long.

2 Loop both the large bubbles and twist the ends together. You should now have two large loops and a straight portion of balloon.

balloon pump

CRAFT TIP

If you get the size of the swan's body just right, you can wear this design as a hat!

3 Tuck one loop inside the other. Arrange the loops carefully to make the swan's body with the wings sticking up at the top.

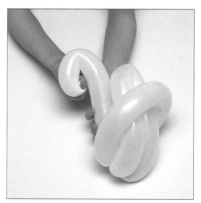

4 To create the elegant curved neck of the swan, pinch the end of the balloon and bend it round.

Spinner

An alternative to the traditional wooden die is this spinning hexagonal version. You could make it with more sides and higher numbers to make board games more exciting. You will need to use simple geometry if you want to make an eight or ten-sided shape.

YOU WILL NEED
tracing paper
pencil
medium-weight card (posterboard)
scissors
thin red paper
thin blue paper
non-toxic paper glue
scraps of coloured paper
thin coloured card (posterboard)

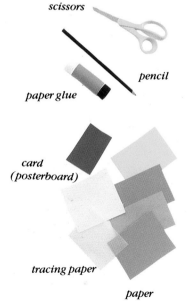

scissors

pencil

paper glue

card (posterboard)

tracing paper

paper

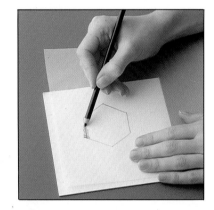

1 Trace the spinner from the template and transfer it to the medium-weight card (posterboard).

2 Cut out the spinner shape and draw around it on red and blue paper. Cut out the shapes you have drawn and stick them to the front and back of the card.

3 Cut thin strips of orange paper and stick them to the red side of the spinner in a star formation to give six sections. Draw the numbers 1 to 6 on scraps of coloured paper, cut them out and stick them in sequence around the spinner.

4 Draw and cut a spinning stick from thin coloured card. Make a small slit in the centre of the spinner and insert the stick through the slit.

Magnetic Fish Game

This is a version of an old and much-loved game that has been played by generations of children. To make the game more competitive, you could write a score on the back of each fish. The player with the highest score wins.

YOU WILL NEED
scraps of heavy coloured paper
pencil
scissors
wax crayons
paper clips
thin wooden sticks
thin coloured cord
small horseshoe magnet

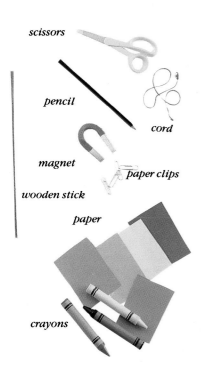

scissors

pencil

cord

magnet

paper clips

wooden stick

paper

crayons

1 Draw fish shapes onto the scraps of paper and cut them out.

2 Decorate the fish using wax crayons.

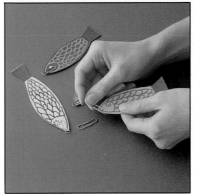

3 Attach a paper clip to the nose of each fish so that it can be picked up by the fishing line.

4 To make the fishing rod, tie a length of cord to the wooden dowel and tie a small magnet to the end of the line.

Stencilled Snap Cards

A game of snap is always good fun. Why not make your own set of cards like this cheerful version? The cards are stencilled with different colours. Each stencil can be used several times if allowed to dry thoroughly between colours. Use a sharp craft knife to cut the stencils: this needs to be done by an adult.

YOU WILL NEED
stencil card (cardboard)
ruler
pencil
scissors
craft knife and cutting mat
heavy paper in four different
    colours
small squares of household sponge
non-toxic paint in four different
    colours
non-toxic paper glue
medium-weight coloured card
    (posterboard)

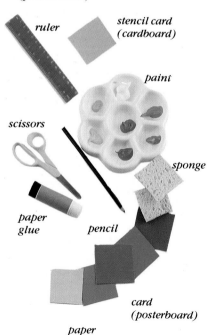

ruler   *stencil card (cardboard)*

paint

scissors

sponge

paper glue   *pencil*

card (posterboard)

paper

1 Cut four pieces of stencil card (cardboard) measuring approximately 6 × 9 cm (2¼ × 3½ in).

2 Draw four different symbols on four pieces of stencil card. Cut out the motifs using a craft knife.

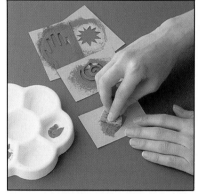

3 Cut rectangles of coloured paper measuring 6.5 × 8.5 cm (2½ × 3¼ in). Place the first stencil on one of the rectangles. With a sponge square, dab paint over the stencil until the cut-out space is covered. Carefully remove the stencil, taking care not to smudge the paint. Repeat with all the stencils until you have made enough cards.

4 Stick each stencilled rectangle onto a slightly larger piece of medium-weight card (posterboard). Allow the glue to dry thoroughly before you play snap.

PLAYING SNAP

To play, deal out all the cards to each player. In turn, discard one card onto a central pile. If two cards of the same pair are played in sequence, the first player to notice must shout 'snap' and grab the pair. The player with the most pairs at the end of the game wins. It sounds simple, but try playing very quickly!

Paper Plate Tennis

A fun game for two or more players to play around the house or outdoors.

YOU WILL NEED
4 paper plates
coloured paints
paintbrush
scissors
coloured sticky-tape
ping-pong ball

paper plate

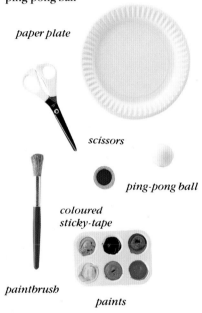

scissors

ping-pong ball

*coloured
sticky-tape*

paintbrush

paints

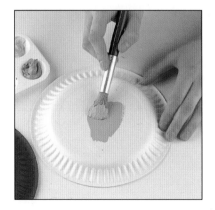

1 For each 'racquet' you will need two paper plates. Paint each plate a plain colour. Allow to dry.

2 Paint patterns onto the plates and leave to dry.

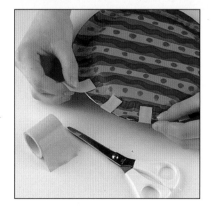

3 Attach the plates with pieces of coloured sticky-tape, leaving a gap big enough for your hand to slide in.

4 Paint the ping-pong ball. Now you are ready to start playing.

Air Soccer

A fun game for two or more players. Use the blowers to move the ball into the opposite goal.

YOU WILL NEED
pencil
scissors
card (cardboard) or 2 shoe boxes
masking tape
coloured paints
paintbrush
coloured sticky-back (adhesive)
   plastic
2 cardboard tubes
ping-pong ball
green sticky-back (adhesive) felt

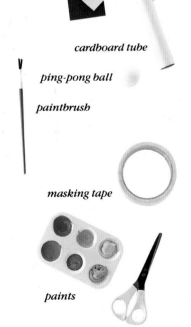

plastic covering

card (cardboard)

cardboard tube

ping-pong ball

paintbrush

masking tape

paints

scissors

1 Draw the goals onto card (cardboard) and cut out with a pair of scissors, or cut one long side off of each shoe box.

2 Bend back the two short sides about 2.5 cm (1 in) so the goal will stand up. Stick the card together with masking tape if necessary.

3 Paint the goals inside and out. Cut out some spots from the coloured sticky-back (adhesive) plastic and stick them onto the goals.

4 For the blowers, cover two cardboard tubes with coloured sticky-back plastic.

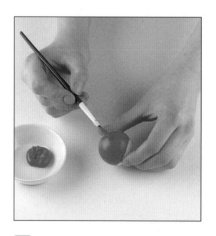

5 Paint the ping-pong ball with bright colours.

6 For the pitch (field), cover a piece of card as big as you like with green sticky-back felt. Mark out the pitch with masking tape and position the goals.

Character Skittles

Plastic bottles make excellent skittles, especially if you paint them to look like people. You can play the game indoors as well as outside if you use a soft ball.

YOU WILL NEED
clean, empty plastic bottles
fretsaw
newspaper
PVA (white) glue and brush
water
paper baubles (balls)
non-toxic strong glue
acrylic paint, in assorted colours
paintbrush
ribbon, in various colours
  and patterns

newspaper

brush

plastic bottle

paper bauble (ball)

PVA (white) glue

ribbon

paint

fretsaw

strong glue

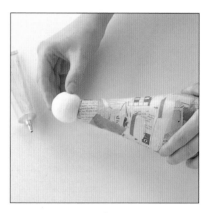

1 Remove the labels from the bottles by soaking them in water. Saw off the top of each bottle as shown.

2 Tear the newspaper into strips and soak in dilute PVA (white) glue. Cover the bottles in papier-mâché and leave to dry.

3 Glue a paper bauble (ball) on top of each bottle, using strong glue.

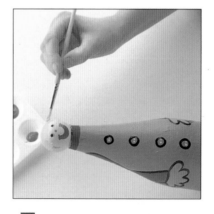

4 Paint the bottles and the bauble faces with a base coat. Leave until the paint is completely dry.

5 Give each skittle a different character by painting different coloured hair and clothes. Leave the second coat of paint to dry.

6 Tie a piece of ribbon in a bow round the neck of each skittle.

Jumbo Dominoes

This is a giant version of a favourite game,
painted in bright colours to make it twice as much
fun. Make as many dominoes as you like –
a traditional set has 28 pieces.

YOU WILL NEED
pine plank 7.5 cm (3 in) wide
ruler
pencil
saw
sandpaper
paint, in assorted colours
paintbrush
sticky black spots
varnish and brush

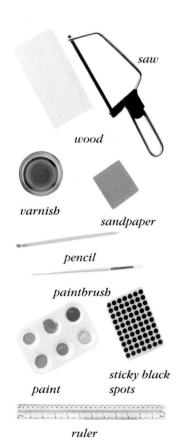

saw

wood

varnish

sandpaper

pencil

paintbrush

paint

sticky black spots

ruler

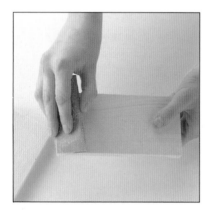

1 Measure 15 cm x 7.5 cm (6 x 3 in)
rectangles on the wood and cut out
carefully. Sand the surfaces and corners
thoroughly until smooth.

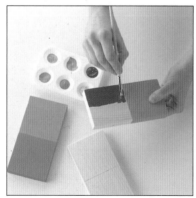

2 Divide each rectangle in half to
make two squares. Paint each half a
different colour, leaving the paint to dry
between each colour.

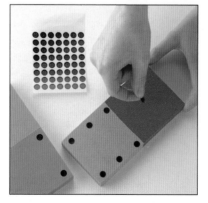

3 Stick black spots on each face of
the dominoes. Vary the number of spots
from zero to six.

4 Finally, varnish the dominoes.

Star Checkerboard

Make your own painted draughts or checkers board then make a set of draughts to play with. Any small pastry cutter shape would be suitable for the pieces.

YOU WILL NEED
52 x 52 cm (20 x 20 in) MDF (fiberboard)
metal ruler
pencil
emulsion (latex) or acrylic paint, in two contrasting colours
paintbrush
masking tape, optional
varnish and brush
polymer clay, in two colours to match board
small star pastry cutter

small star pastry cutter

MDF (fiberboard)

pencil

acrylic paint

metal ruler

polymer clay

varnish

paintbrush

masking tape

1 Using a ruler, divide the wood into 64 squares, each measuring 6.5 x 6.5 cm (2½ x 2½ in).

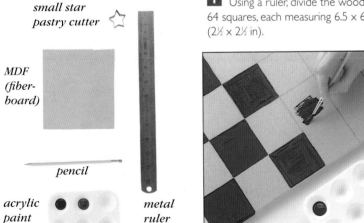

2 Paint alternate squares in the first colour. To help paint straight lines, you can mark out the squares with masking tape and remove it when the paint is completely dry.

3 Paint the remaining squares with the second colour. When completely dry, apply a coat of varnish.

4 For the pieces, roll the polymer clay to approximately 5 mm (¼ in) thick. Using the pastry cutter, cut out 12 shapes from each colour. Bake, following the manufacturer's instructions, and allow to cool.

Tic-Tac-Toe

This old favourite has been brought up to date with bright jazzy colours. It can be a fast and furious game, so you could play a knock-out tournament at your party, with a prize for the champion.

YOU WILL NEED
medium-weight card (posterboard)
ruler
pencil
scissors
thick pink, yellow, green and blue
    paper
non-toxic paper glue

pencil

scissors

ruler

paper

paper glue

*card
(posterboard)*

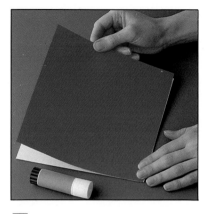

2 Place the cardboard square on the pink paper and draw around it. Cut out the paper square and stick it to the card.

3 Cut a smaller square of card measuring 15 × 15 cm (6 × 6 in). Cut a piece of yellow paper the same size.

1 Mark out a square measuring 20 × 20 cm (8 × 8 in) on medium-weight card (posterboard). Cut out the square.

4 Stick the yellow paper to the card and cut the card into nine squares each measuring 5 × 5 cm (2 × 2 in).

5 Cut four strips of green paper 15 × 1 cm (6 × ⅜ in). Stick them to the pink board to form nine equal squares.

6 Draw noughts and crosses (X's and O's) on the pink and blue paper. Cut them out and stick them to the yellow squares to complete the cards.

Jigsaw Puzzle

Challenge the skills of your party guests with this home-made jigsaw puzzle.

YOU WILL NEED
colourful picture or large photograph
  of your choice
card (cardboard)
PVA (white) glue
scissors
pencil
paintbrush

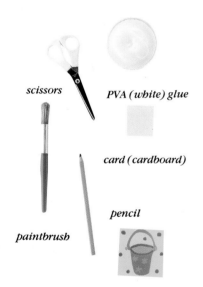

scissors

PVA (white) glue

card (cardboard)

pencil

paintbrush

picture

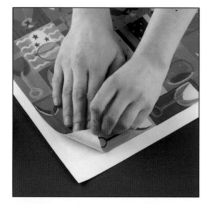

I Stick your picture onto a piece of card (cardboard) with PVA (white) glue. Rub the palm of your hand over the picture to make sure it is completely smooth. Allow it to dry.

2 Cut around the picture with a pair of scissors to remove the excess card.

CRAFT HINT
You could cut out a picture from a magazine rather than using a photograph.

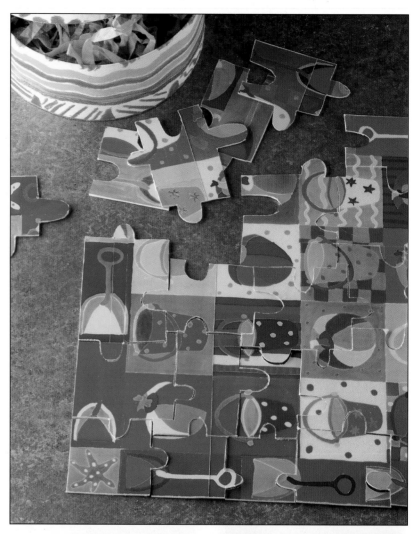

3 Draw the jigsaw pieces onto the reverse of the picture with a pencil.

4 Carefully cut out the jigsaw shapes and keep them in a safe place.

Juggling Squares

A brilliant juggling act could form part of the party entertainment. Make your own squares.

YOU WILL NEED
squares of colourful fabric
pencil
ruler
scissors
pins
needle
thread
crumpled paper or newspaper

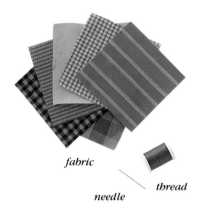

fabric

needle   *thread*

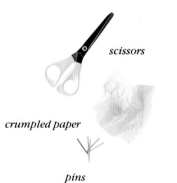

scissors

crumpled paper

pins

IMPORTANT SAFETY NOTE
You may need an adult's help for the sewing.

1 For each juggling square you will need six squares of fabric, 12 x 12 cm (4¾ x 4¾ in). Cut these out with a pair of scissors. With the right sides facing each other sew the first two squares together with a needle and thread, allowing a 1 cm (½ in) seam allowance.

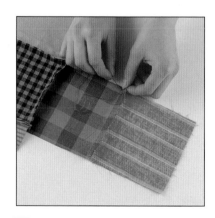

2 Sew all the squares together to form a letter 'T' shape.

3 Join the sides together to form a cube, leaving one side open for the stuffing. Turn the cube right side out.

4 Fill the cube with the crumpled paper or newspaper, and, when it is full, sew up the last side.

Catch-the-ball Game

Test everyone's skill with this bat-and-ball game. It takes quite a lot of practice to catch the ball in the cup but it's good fun while you are learning! Use a plastic bottle with a long neck, because this makes a better handle to hold onto.

YOU WILL NEED
coloured tissue paper
PVA (white) glue
mixing container
clear plastic bottle
scissors
yogurt pot
strong, non-toxic glue
thin coloured cord

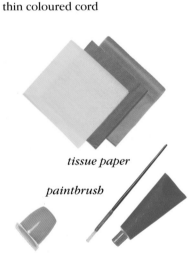

tissue paper

paintbrush

yogurt pot   *strong glue*

cord

plastic bottle

1 Take two sheets of differently coloured tissue paper and tear them into strips and circles.

2 Mix some PVA (white) glue with a little water. Coat each strip of paper with glue. Cover the bottle with the paper. Add some circles of paper on top of the strips. Leave to dry thoroughly.

3 Carefully cut the corners from the top of the yogurt pot. Glue the pot to the centre of the bottle.

4 Roll a sheet of tissue paper tightly into a small ball. It should be small enough to fit inside the yogurt pot.

5 Cut a long piece of coloured cord. Tie one end of the cord tightly around the ball of tissue paper.

6 Tie the other end of the thin coloured cord around the end of the neck of the bottle.

Missing Money Trick

This trick will amaze the party guests. It's every magician's favourite, because it cannot go wrong. All you need are five coins and some sticky tape fixed to the palm of your hand. Keep the palm of your hand concealed during the trick, otherwise the audience will work out your secret.

YOU WILL NEED
5 small coins of the same size
strong, clear sticky tape

5 small coins of the same size

sticky tape

I Cut a small piece of sticky tape. Overlap the ends, sticky side out, to make a loop. Firmly press the loop of tape onto the palm of your hand.

2 Place the five coins in front of you on the table. Make a show of counting the five coins one-by-one as you stack them one on top of the other. Ask the audience to count along with you.

CRAFT TIP

In place of a loop of sticky tape you can use a small piece of double-sided tape. Use small coins rather than large ones. You can use plastic coins, if you like.

3 Press the hand with the sticky loop onto the pile of coins. Say some magic words and then withdraw your hand and place it flat on the table. Spread out the pile of coins and count them out loud.

4 There are now only four coins. You, of course, know that the fifth coin is stuck in the palm of your hand. Remove it when you return the other coins to your pocket.

Quick Separation

This game will really test your hand and eye co-ordination. The aim is to separate a stack of draughts (checkers) pieces into two piles in the shortest time possible. Challenge your party guests to a friendly game: you will need to ask someone to be time-keeper. Good luck!

YOU WILL NEED
4 black and 4 white draughts
  (checkers) pieces
ruler
watch or clock with a
  seconds hand

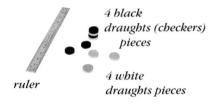

ruler

*4 black
draughts (checkers)
pieces*

*4 white
draughts pieces*

1 Stack the draughts (checkers) pieces one on top of the other, alternating black and white. Challenge everyone to separate the stack into a black pile and a white pile in the shortest time possible. No matter how quick they are, you will be quicker.

CRAFT TIP
If you want to make this game a bit more challenging, increase the number of draughts (checkers) pieces in the stack. Be warned – the taller the stack, the easier it is to knock over.

2 This is how you do it. Hold the ruler flat on the table next to the stack of draughts pieces. Then quickly flick the ruler from side to side. The black pieces will go to one side and the white pieces to the other side.

3 The pieces will fly everywhere if your technique is not right. If you flick the ruler too slowly, the stack will topple over. If you flick the ruler too much, two or three pieces will fly off at the same time. There is only one way to get it right – keep on practising.

Shaker

Young children will enjoy making and playing their own musical instruments at your party.

YOU WILL NEED
clear plastic bottle, with cap
small beads and buttons
large and small coloured
    sticky-paper dots
strong, non-toxic glue

sticky-paper dots

buttons and beads   *glue*

1 Wash and carefully dry the bottle. It should be dry inside as well. Pour a mixture of small beads and buttons into the bottle. A couple of handfuls will make a good noise.

2 Spread a line of glue around the inside of the bottle top. Screw the top back onto the bottle. Stick coloured sticky-paper dots to the outside to make a bright and decorative pattern.

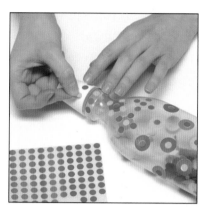

3 Stick a row of small coloured sticky-paper dots around the lower edge of the bottle top to make a pattern.

Tambourine

Two foil pie dishes can quickly and easily become a shiny tambourine.

YOU WILL NEED
ruler
thin satin ribbon
scissors
small bells
sticky tape
2 foil pie-dishes (pans)
strong, non-toxic glue

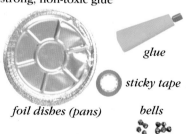

glue

sticky tape

foil dishes (pans)   *bells*

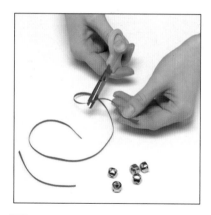

1 Cut 10 cm (3 in) lengths of ribbon and tie a bell to each piece.

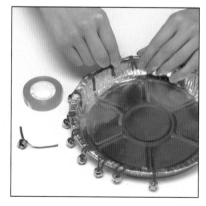

2 Tape the bells around the inside edge of one of the pie dishes (pans), making sure you space them evenly.

3 Spread glue around the rim of the second pie dish. Glue the two dishes together, rim to rim, covering the ends of the ribbons. Leave the glue to dry.

PARTY FOOD AND DRINKS

This is the most important part of the party, and your kids will love choosing from the exciting suggestions in this chapter. Many of the recipes are simple enough for them to follow themselves, with supervision and just a little help.

There are lots of ideas for irresistible finger food and interesting things on sticks, as well as new twists on standard kids' favourites such as pizzas and burgers. There are some great recipes for drinks, too.

During the meal, offer plenty to drink, as everyone will be thirsty after all the games, and keep passing round the plates of food so that no one misses out. If you're serving hot food, let it cool a little before you put it on the table.

Working Tools

The children will be keen to help to make all the exciting things they have chosen for their party meal, so it's a good time to teach them how to use the equipment they'll need.

Food processor
This is actually a giant blender, with a large bowl and, usually, lots of attachments. The metal chopping blade is the one we use most; it's best with dry ingredients like vegetables and pastry. The plastic blade is for batters and cakes. Some processors also have grating blades and slicing plates.

Electric whisk
A whisk's main function is to beat in air and make the mixture bigger and thicker, as in, for example, cream and cake mixtures. But a whisk can also blend such things as sauces together and make them very smooth.

Blenders
Also called liquidizers, these are usually attached to an electric whisk motor or a food processor and are tall and deep, with blades at the base. Ideal for turning things into liquid such as fruit for sauces, soups and milk shakes. Hand-held blenders are much smaller and can be used in a small bowl or mug.

Safety first for whisks, blenders and processors
Never put your hand in the processor to move something while it is plugged in. And keep small fingers away from whisks while they are whizzing round.

Treat all electrical equipment very carefully and unplug everything before you fiddle around with blades.

Chopping (cutting) boards
Lots of people use the same board for all their preparation, but it's much more hygienic to use a different one for each type of job. It is possible to buy boards with coloured handles, so the same one is always used for the same job. A wooden board is best for cutting bread. Scrub boards well after use.

Graters
A pyramid-shaped or box-shaped grater is the most useful type. Each side has a different grating surface, made up of small, curved, raised blades. Use the coarsest one for vegetables and cheese and the finer sides for grating orange and lemon rind. Stand the grater on a flat surface while you use it. The grated food will collect inside. Scrub well with a brush after use. There are also very small graters available for whole nutmegs.

Measuring equipment
Most homes have some sort of measuring equipment, whether scales, spoons or cups. The recipes in this book give both metric and imperial weights, such as 115g/4oz.

These are not always exact equivalents but have been rounded either up or down to convenient amounts. If you mix the two systems, the recipe may not work correctly. Choose either system: as long as you stick to the same ones for each recipe, you shouldn't have any problems.

There are three measurements to choose from for liquids. The metric measurement, such as 300 ml, is followed by ½ pint – the imperial one; and, finally, 1¼ cups, which is the American measure. Most measuring jugs or cups have all these measurements written on the side for easy measuring.

Small amounts of both dry and wet ingredients are often measured in millilitres (ml) and tablespoons (tbsp). 15 ml is the same as 1 tbsp and 5 ml is the same as 1 teaspoon (1 tsp). The spoon should be level.

Bowls
Mixing bowls come in all sorts of sizes, and the most useful ones are made from heatproof glass. Use large ones for pastry, bread-making, whisking egg whites and mixing cake mixtures; smaller ones are better for smaller quantities, such as beating eggs and mixing dips.

Pans
Saucepans and frying pans can be made from different metals; some are even made of glass! The most popular are stainless steel pans and aluminium ones. Pans need to have a thick base to stop food from sticking. Large pans can be very heavy, so an adult may need to help with lifting and pouring.

colander

nutmeg grater

baking tray

bun tin

saucepans

saucepan

springform
cake tins

frying pan

wire cooling rack

grater

muffin
tin

measuring cups

whisks

weighing scales

food processor

mixing bowls

electric blender

measuring
spoons

chopping boards

measuring jug

Egg People

The kids can grow their own cress (watercress) for party sandwiches by making these great characters with green hair that grows.

YOU WILL NEED
eggs
bowl
cotton wool (ball)
water
cress (watercress) seeds
coloured paints
paintbrush

paintbrush

cress (watercress) seeds

egg

cotton wool (ball)

paints

1 Carefully take the tops off the eggs and empty the contents into a bowl.

2 Moisten a piece of cotton wool (ball) in cold water and place it inside each empty egg shell.

3 Sprinkle the cress (watercress) seeds sparingly into the shells. Store the egg shells in a dark place for 2 days or until the seeds have sprouted, then transfer to a light area such as a windowsill.

4 Keep the eggs moist but do not overwater them. The cress should take a few days to grow. Paint a jolly face onto each egg shell.

COOK'S TIP

Save the shells when you are cooking with eggs, and make some egg people to decorate the party table.

Tasty Toasts

Finger food is perfect for parties, and these toasts look colourful and appetizing. They're sophisticated enough to appeal to all ages.

Makes 8

INGREDIENTS
2 red (bell) peppers, halved
  lengthways and seeded
30 ml/2 tbsp sunflower oil
1 garlic clove, crushed
1 short French stick
45 ml/3 tbsp pesto
50 g/2 oz/⅓ cup soft goat's cheese

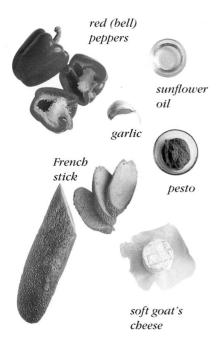

red (bell)
peppers

sunflower
oil

garlic

French
stick

pesto

soft goat's
cheese

1 Put the (bell) pepper halves, cut-side down, under a hot grill (broiler) until the skins blacken, then transfer them to a plastic bag, tie the top and leave them to cool. Peel off the skins, discard the seeds and cut the peppers into strips.

2 Put the oil in a small bowl and stir in the crushed garlic. Cut the bread diagonally into slices and brush one side of each slice with the garlic-flavoured oil. Arrange the slices on a grill pan and brown under a hot grill (broiler).

3 Turn the slices over. Brush the untoasted sides with the garlic-flavoured oil, then spread with the pesto.

4 Arrange pepper strips over each slice and put small wedges of goat's cheese on top. Grill (broil) again until the cheese has browned and melted slightly. Serve hot or cold.

VARIATION

For children who don't like pesto, substitute home-made tomato sauce. Brown an onion in a little oil, add a can of chopped tomatoes with basil, stir in a generous dollop of tomato purée (paste) and add a pinch of sugar. Simmer until thick and tasty.

Pizza Faces

These funny faces are very easy to make. The base is a crispy crumpet (English muffin) topped with tomato sauce and melted cheese. Use what you like to create the shapes for the smiley faces.

Makes 9

INGREDIENTS

30 ml/2 tbsp vegetable oil
1 onion, finely shredded
220 g/1 x 7 oz can chopped
 tomatoes
25 g/1 oz tomato purée (paste)
salt and pepper
9 crumpets (English muffins)
1 x 200 g/7 oz packet of processed
 cheese slices
1 green pepper, seeded and
 chopped into small pieces
4–5 sliced cherry
 tomatoes

*crumpet
(English muffin)*

onion

*tomato purée
(paste)*

cheese slices

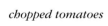
chopped tomatoes

1 Preheat the oven to 220°C/425°F/Gas 7. Heat the oil in a large pan, add the onion and cook for about 2–3 minutes, until softened.

2 Add the can of tomatoes, tomato purée (paste) and salt and pepper. Bring to a boil and cook for 5–6 minutes until the mixture becomes thick and pulpy. Leave to cool.

3 Lightly toast the crumpets (English muffins) under the grill (broiler). Lay them on a baking (cookie) sheet. Put a heaped teaspoonful of the tomato mixture on the top and spread it out evenly. Bake in the preheated oven for 25 minutes.

4 Cut the cheese slices into strips and arrange them with the green pepper and the cherry tomatoes on top of the pizzas to make smiley faces. Return to the oven for about 5 minutes until the cheese melts. Serve the pizzas while still warm.

Homeburgers

These burgers hide a delicious surprise – a soft, cheesy centre. Serve them with chips (french fries) and a crisp green salad.

Makes 4

INGREDIENTS
450 g/1 lb lean minced
  (ground) beef
2 slices of bread, crusts removed
1 egg
4 spring onions (scallions),
  roughly chopped
1 garlic clove, peeled and chopped
15 ml/1 tbsp mango chutney
10 ml/2 tsp dried mixed herbs
50 g/2 oz/⅓ cup mozzarella cheese
salt and pepper
4 burger buns, to serve

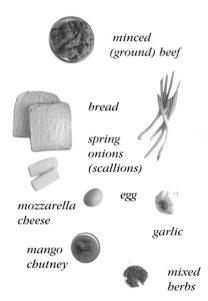

minced (ground) beef

bread

spring onions (scallions)

mozzarella cheese

egg

garlic

mango chutney

mixed herbs

1 Put the beef, bread, egg, spring onions (scallions) and garlic in a food processor. Add a little salt and pepper and whizz until evenly blended. Add the chutney and herbs and whizz again.

2 Divide the mixture into four equal portions. With damp hands, to stop the meat from sticking, pat into flat rounds.

3 Cut the cheese into four equal pieces and put one in the centre of each round. Wrap the meat round the cheese to make a fat burger. Chill for 30 minutes. Preheat the grill (broiler).

4 Put the burgers on a rack under the hot grill (broiler), but not too close or they will burn on the outside before the middle has cooked properly. Cook them for 5–8 minutes on each side, then put each burger in a bun to serve.

Wicked Tortilla Wedges

A tortilla is a thick omelette with lots of cooked potatoes in it. It can be eaten hot or cold, but is nicest warm. Cut into chunky wedges, it makes great party food.

Makes 6

INGREDIENTS
30 ml/2 tbsp sunflower oil
675 g/1½ lb potatoes, cut in small chunks
1 onion, sliced
115 g/4 oz/1½ cups mushrooms, sliced
115 g/4 oz/1 cup frozen peas, thawed
50 g/2 oz/⅓ cup frozen sweetcorn (corn) kernels, thawed
4 eggs
150 ml/¼ pint/⅔ cup milk
30 ml/2 tbsp chopped fresh parsley
salt (optional)

sunflower oil

potatoes

onion

mushrooms

peas

eggs

sweetcorn (corn)

milk

Cajun seasoning (optional)

fresh parsley

COOK'S TIP
Make sure the frying pan can be safely used under the grill (broiler). Shield wooden handles with foil.

1 Heat the oil in a large frying pan and fry the potatoes and onion for 3–4 minutes, stirring often. Lower the heat, cover the pan and fry gently for 8–10 minutes more, until the potatoes are almost tender.

2 Add the mushrooms to the pan and cook for 2–3 minutes more, stirring often, until they have softened.

3 Add the peas and sweetcorn (corn) and stir them into the potato mixture.

4 Put the eggs and milk in a bowl. Add the Cajun seasoning and a little salt, if you like; beat well.

5 Level the top of the vegetables and scatter the parsley on top. Pour on the egg mixture and cook over a low heat for 10–15 minutes.

6 Put the pan under a hot grill (broiler) to set the top of the tortilla. Serve hot or cold, cut into wedges.

Roly Poly Porcupines

Everyone loves frankfurter sausages (hot dogs), and they're especially good if skewered into hot baked potatoes. Serve with a bowl of tomato ketchup nearby.

Makes 4

INGREDIENTS
4 large baking potatoes
6–8 frankfurter sausages (hot dogs)
50 g/2 oz cherry tomatoes
50 g/2 oz mild Cheddar cheese
2 sticks celery
toothpicks
iceberg lettuce, shredded
small pieces of red pepper and
  black olive
1 carrot, chopped

potato

celery

*cherry
tomatoes*

*frankfurter
sausages (hot
dogs)*

Cheddar cheese

1 Preheat the oven to 200°C/400°F/ Gas 6. Scrub the potatoes and prick them all over. Bake for 1–1¼ hours until soft (test with a skewer).

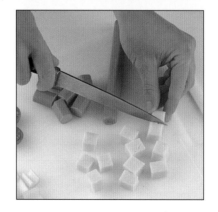

2 Meanwhile, prepare the frankfurters (hot dogs). Heat the frankfurter sausages in a large pan of boiling water for 8–10 minutes until they are warmed through. Drain and leave to cool slightly.

3 Cut the cherry tomatoes in half and, when cool enough to handle, chop the sausages into 2.5 cm (1 in) pieces. Cut the cheese into cubes and slice the celery. Spear the chunks of food ontoothpicks in different combinations.

4 When the potatoes are cooked, remove them from the oven. Pierce the skin all over with the toothpicks topped with the frankfurters, cheese cubes, cherry tomatoes and celery slices. Serve on shredded lettuce and decorate each porcupine's head with pieces of red pepper and olive, and a carrot snout.

Nutty Chicken Kebabs

A tasty Thai dish that's quick to make and uses everyone's favourite spread in the dip.

Makes 12

INGREDIENTS
30 ml/2 tbsp oil
15 ml/1 tbsp lemon juice
450 g/1 lb boneless, skinless
    chicken breasts, cut in
    small cubes

FOR THE DIP
5 ml/1 tsp chilli powder
75 ml/5 tbsp water
15 ml/1 tbsp oil
1 small onion, grated
1 garlic clove, peeled and crushed
30 ml/2 tbsp lemon juice
60 ml/4 tbsp crunchy peanut butter
5 ml/1 tsp salt
5 ml/1 tsp ground coriander
sliced cucumber and lemon
    wedges, to serve

lemon juice

crunchy peanut butter

onion

oil

chilli powder

chicken

ground coriander

garlic

1 Soak 12 wooden skewers in water, to prevent them from burning during grilling (broiling). Combine the oil and lemon juice in a bowl and stir in the cubed chicken. Cover and leave to marinate for at least 30 minutes.

2 Thread four or five cubes on each wooden skewer. Cook under a hot grill (broiler), turning often, for about ten minutes, or until cooked and browned. Cut one piece open to check that it is cooked right through: this is very important with chicken.

3 Meanwhile, make the dip. Mix the chilli powder with 15 ml/1 tbsp of the water. Heat the oil in a small frying pan and fry the onion and garlic until tender.

CAUTION
This recipe is not suitable for children with nut allergies.

4 Turn down the heat and add the chilli paste and the remaining ingredients and stir well. Stir in more water if the sauce is too thick. Put the sauce into a small bowl and serve warm, with the chicken kebabs, cucumber slices and lemon wedges.

Crispy Potato Skins

Appetizing baked potato skins, served with a delicious spicy dip.

Makes 32

INGREDIENTS
8 large potatoes, scrubbed
30–45 ml/2–3 tbsp oil
90 ml/6 tbsp mayonnaise
30 ml/2 tbsp natural (plain) yogurt
5 ml/1 tsp curry paste
30 ml/2 tbsp roughly chopped fresh
  coriander (cilantro)
salt

curry paste

potatoes

mayonnaise

*fresh coriander
(cilantro)*

natural (plain) yogurt

1 Preheat the oven to 190°C/375°F/ Gas 5. Arrange the potatoes in a roasting tin (pan), prick them all over with a fork and cook for 45 minutes or until tender. Leave to cool slightly.

2 Carefully cut each potato into quarters lengthways, holding it with a clean tea towel (dish towel) if it's still a bit hot.

3 Scoop out some of the centre with a knife or spoon and put the skins back in the roasting tin. Save the cooked potato for another dish.

4 Brush the skins with oil and sprinkle with salt before putting them back in the oven. Cook for 30–40 minutes more, until they are crisp and brown, brushing them occasionally with more oil.

5 Meanwhile, put the mayonnaise, yogurt, curry paste and 1 tbsp coriander (cilantro) in a small bowl and mix together well. Leave for 30–40 minutes for the flavour to develop.

6 Put the dip in a clean bowl and arrange the skins around the edge. Serve hot, sprinkled with the remaining coriander (cilantro).

Bacon Twists

Home-baked bread and crispy bacon make a brilliant combination, and these will disappear fast. Serve with a bowl of soft cheese with herbs.

Makes 12

INGREDIENTS
450 g/1 lb/4 cups strong (enriched) white flour
6 g/¼ oz easy-blend (active dry) yeast
2.5 ml/½ tsp salt
400 ml/14 fl oz/1¾ cups warm water
12 streaky bacon rashers (strips)
1 egg, beaten

water

flour

egg

yeast

salt

bacon

1 Mix the flour, yeast and salt in a bowl and stir them together. Add a little of the water and mix with a knife. Add the remaining water and use your hands to pull the mixture together, to make a sticky dough.

2 Turn the dough onto a lightly floured surface and knead it for 5 minutes, or until the dough is smooth and stretchy.

3 Divide into 12 pieces and roll each one into a sausage shape.

4 Lay each bacon rasher (strip) on a chopping board and run the back of the knife down its length, to stretch it slightly. Wind a piece of bacon round each dough "sausage".

5 Brush the "sausages" with beaten egg and arrange them on a lightly oiled baking (cookie) sheet. Leave somewhere warm for 30 minutes, or until they have doubled in size. Preheat the oven to 200°C/400°F/Gas 6 and cook the "sausages" for 20–25 minutes, until cooked and browned.

COOK'S TIP
Tap the base of a breadstick to see if it is ready – if it sounds hollow, it's cooked.

Bread Zoo

Get all the children to shape their own bread
animals, and bake them in time for the party meal.

Makes 15

INGREDIENTS
2 x 275 g/10 oz packets white
   bread mix
oil, for greasing
a few currants
½ small red (bell) pepper
1 small carrot
beaten egg, to glaze

bread mix   *currants*

carrot

red (bell)   *egg*
pepper

oil

1 Put the bread mix in a large bowl
and make up according to the
manufacturer's instructions. When it is a
pliable dough, knead it on a lightly
floured surface for 5 minutes until it is
smooth and elastic. Return the dough to
the bowl, cover with oiled clear film
(plastic wrap) and leave in a warm place
for ¾–1 hour until it has doubled in bulk.

2 Knead the dough again for 5 minutes
and divide into five pieces. Cut one piece
of dough into three and shape each into
a 15 cm/6 in snake, making a slit for the
mouth. Twist the snakes on a greased
baking (cookie) sheet and add currant
eyes. Slice a thin strip of (bell) pepper,
cutting a triangle at one end for the
forked tongue.

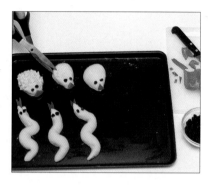

3 For hedgehogs, take another piece
of dough and cut into three. Shape each
into an oval about 6 cm/2¼ in long. Place
on the baking sheet and add currant eyes
and a red pepper nose. Snip the dough
with scissors to make the prickly spines.

4 To make mice, take a third piece of
dough and cut into four pieces. Shape
three pieces into ovals each about 6
cm/2¼ in long and place on the baking
sheet. Shape tiny rounds of dough for
ears and wiggly tails from the fourth
piece of dough. Press onto the mice
bodies and use the currants for eyes, and
small strips of carrot for whiskers.

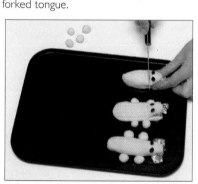

5 For crocodiles, cut another piece of
dough into three. Take a small piece off
each and reserve. Shape the large pieces
into 10 cm/4 in long sausages. Make slits
for the mouths and wedge open with
crumpled foil. Add currant eyes. Shape
the spare dough into feet and press into
position. Make criss-cross cuts on the
backs for scales.

6 To make rabbits, cut the remaining
dough into three. Take a small piece off
each for tails. Roll the main pieces into
thick sausages, 18 cm/7 in long. Loop the
dough and twist twice to form the body
and head of the rabbit. Use the rest for
tails. Preheat the oven to 220°C/425°F/
Gas 7. Cover all with oiled clear film
(plastic wrap) and leave in a warm place
for 12 minutes. Brush with beaten egg
and cook for 10–12 minutes until golden.

COOK'S TIP

Bread mixes are a fast and easy way
to make bread, and although you
are more restricted with the types of
bread you can make, the results are
just as delicious. You can find mixes
in most supermarkets.

Cheese Straws

These delicious cheese sticks melt in the mouth and will jump off the plate as soon as you put them on the table. The sticks are ideal for eating with dips, but you could also make different shapes with some cookie cutters.

Makes about 60

INGREDIENTS
little oil, for greasing
175 g/6 oz/1½ cups plain (all-purpose) flour
75 g/3 oz/6 tbsp butter or margarine, cut into pieces
115 g/4 oz/1 cup grated Cheddar cheese
1 egg, beaten

flour

butter

egg

grated Cheddar cheese

oil

1 Preheat the oven to 200°C/400°F/ Gas 6. Lightly brush two baking (cookie) sheets with oil. Place the flour in a bowl and rub in the butter or margarine.

2 Stir the grated Cheddar cheese into the flour mixture. Reserve 15 ml/1 tbsp beaten egg for glazing and stir the rest into the mixture too. Mix to a smooth dough, adding a little water if necessary.

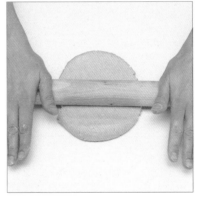

3 Knead lightly, then roll out on a floured surface to a 30 × 20 cm/12 × 8 in rectangle. Brush with the remaining beaten egg.

4 Cut into 7.5 × 1 cm/3 × ½ in strips and space slightly apart on the baking sheets. Bake for 8–10 minutes until golden brown. Loosen from, but leave to cool on the baking sheets.

VARIATION
Sprinkle the cheese pastry with extra grated cheese before cutting out the straws, for an extra-strong cheesy taste.

Peanut Cookies

Make sure some of these nutty treats are on the menu for your party, but do check first to see that there are no children with nut allergies.

Makes 25

INGREDIENTS
225 g/8 oz/1 cup butter
30 ml/2 tbsp smooth peanut butter
115 g/4 oz/1 cup icing
  (confectioners') sugar
50 g/2 oz/scant ½ cup cornflour
  (cornstarch)
225 g/8 oz/2 cups plain
  (all-purpose) flour
115 g/4 oz/1 cup unsalted
  peanuts

flour

*cornflour
(cornstarch)*

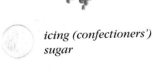

*peanut
butter*

butter

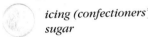

*unsalted
peanuts*

*icing (confectioners')
sugar*

1 Put the butter and peanut butter in a bowl and beat together. Add the sugar, cornflour (cornstarch) and flour and combine with your hands to make a soft and pliable dough.

2 Preheat the oven to 180°C/350°F/ Gas 4 and lightly oil two baking (cookie) sheets. Roll the mixture into 25 small balls, using floured hands, and place the balls on the two baking sheets. Leave plenty of room for the cookies to spread as they cook.

3 Press the tops of the balls of dough flat, using the back of a fork.

4 Press some peanuts into each of the cookies. Cook for 15–20 minutes, until lightly browned. Leave to cool for a few minutes before lifting the cookies carefully onto a wire rack using a palette knife (spatula). When they are cool, store them in an airtight container.

COOK'S TIP
Make really monster cookies by making bigger balls of dough. Leave plenty of room on the baking sheets for them to spread, though.

Kooky Cookies

Cut out these easy cookies in lots of different shapes and let your imagination run wild with the decorating, using bright colours and lots of patterns.

Makes 20

YOU WILL NEED

115 g/4 oz/1 cup self-raising (rising) flour

5 ml/1 tsp ground ginger

5 ml/1 tsp bicarbonate of soda (baking soda)

50 g/4 tbsp sugar

50 g/2 oz/4 tbsp softened butter

30 ml/2 tbsp golden syrup (light corn syrup)

ICING

115 g/4 oz/8 tbsp softened butter

225 g/8 oz/2 cups sifted icing (confectioners') sugar

5 ml/ 1 tsp lemon juice

few drops of food colouring

coloured writing icing (tubes of frosting)

coloured sweets (candies)

sugar

flour

butter

golden syrup (light corn syrup

ginger

icing (confectioners') sugar

1 Sift the flour, ginger and bicarbonate of soda (baking soda) into a bowl. Add the sugar, then rub in the butter with your fingertips until the mixture resembles fine breadcrumbs.

2 Add the golden syrup (light corn syrup) and mix to a dough. Preheat the oven to 190°C/375°F/Gas 5.

3 Roll out to 3 mm/⅛ in thick on a lightly floured surface. Stamp out the shapes with biscuit (cookie) cutters and transfer to a lightly greased baking sheet. Bake for 5–10 minutes before transferring to a wire rack to cool.

4 To make the icing, beat the butter in a bowl until light and fluffy. Add the icing (confectioners') sugar a little at a time and continue beating. Add lemon juice and food colouring.

5 Spread the icing over the cooled cookies and leave to set.

6 When the icing has set make patterns on the cookies with coloured icing (frosting) and decorate with coloured sweets (candies).

Jolly Orange Boats

These are so easy to make and fun to eat. The only difficult thing is waiting for the jelly (gelatin) to set! These boats make an unusual party treat, and they are perfect for a party with a pirate theme.

Makes 8

YOU WILL NEED
2 oranges
1 packet orange-flavoured jelly (gelatin)
rice paper or coloured paper
toothpicks

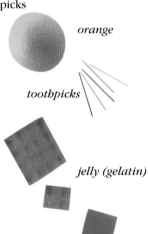

orange

toothpicks

jelly (gelatin)

rice paper

1 Cut the oranges in half lengthwise. Scrape out the flesh, taking care not to pierce the skins. Chop up the flesh.

2 Make the jelly (gelatin) according to the instructions. Add the orange flesh while the jelly cools.

3 Place the orange shells on a baking sheet and pour in the jelly mixture. Leave for at least 1 hour to set. Once set, cut the skins in half again, using a sharp knife, to create little boats.

4 Cut the rice paper or coloured paper sheets into eight squares. Pierce each corner with a toothpick and attach the sail to the middle of the orange boat.

COOK'S TIP

Make sure the orange shells don't wobble on the baking sheet: support them with some crumpled foil if necessary.

Chocolate Witchy Apples

If you're having a party around Halloween, be sure to make these spooky and delicious variations on traditional toffee apples.

Makes 6

YOU WILL NEED
6 small apples
6 wooden skewers
250 g/8 oz/8 squares milk chocolate
6 ice cream cones
sweets (candies) for decorating

apple

milk chocolate

sweets (candies)

wooden skewer

ice cream cone

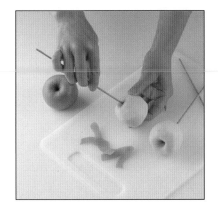

1 Peel and thoroughly dry the apples. Press a wooden skewer into the core of each one.

2 Heat the chocolate in a small bowl over a pan of boiling water until melted.

3 When melted, tilt the pan and dip the apple into it, coating it thoroughly. Place it on a baking (cookie) sheet lined with baking paper (parchment paper). Press the sweets (candies) into the chocolate before the chocolate sets.

4 Holding the stick, use a little melted chocolate to attach the cone for a hat. The cone can also be decorated by sticking sweets on with spare melted chocolate. Repeat with the other apples.

Chocolate Brownies

These classic chewy chocolate bars taste fantastic
with vanilla ice cream.

Makes 9

INGREDIENTS
65 g/2½ oz/⅓ cup butter
50 g/2 oz plain (semi-sweet)
  chocolate
150 g/5 oz/scant 1 cup brown sugar
2 eggs, beaten
65 g/2½ oz/generous ½ cup
  plain (all-purpose) flour
50 g/2 oz/½ cup roughly chopped
  pecans or walnuts
25 g/1 oz/¼ cup icing
  (confectioners') sugar

icing
(confectioners')
sugar

brown
sugar

flour

butter

eggs

plain
(semi-sweet)
chocolate

pecans

1 Put the butter and chocolate in a bowl and stand it over a saucepan of hot, but not boiling, water. Make sure the water doesn't touch the bowl. Leave until the ingredients have melted and then stir them together.

2 Stir the brown sugar into the butter and chocolate mixture and leave for a while to cool slightly.

3 Cut a piece of baking paper (parchment paper) or greaseproof (waxed) paper to fit into the base of an 18 cm/7 in square cake tin (pan).

4 Preheat the oven to 180°C/350°F/ Gas 4. Beat the eggs into the chocolate mixture, then stir in the flour and nuts.

5 Pour the mixture into the lined cake tin and level the top. Cook for 25–35 minutes, until firm around the edges but still slightly soft in the middle.

6 Cut into nine squares and leave to cool in the tin. Dust with a little icing (confectioners') sugar.

Fruit Punch & Fruit Kebabs

Fruit punch is just the ticket on a sultry summer's day, served with mouth-watering fruit kebabs.

Serves 6

INGREDIENTS
FOR THE FRUIT PUNCH
300 ml/¹/₂ pint/1¹/₄ cups orange juice
300 ml/¹/₂ pint/1¹/₄ cups
  pineapple juice
300 ml/¹/₂ pint/1¹/₄ cups tropical fruit
  juice
475 ml/16 fl oz/2 cups lemonade
  fresh pineapple slices and fresh
  cherries, to decorate

FOR THE FRUIT KEBABS
24 small strawberries
24 green seedless grapes
12 marshmallows
1 kiwi fruit, peeled and cut in
  12 wedges
1 banana
15 ml/1 tbsp lemon juice

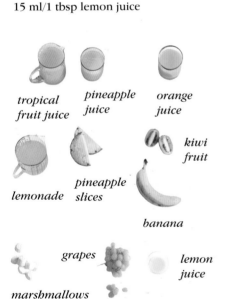

tropical fruit juice   *pineapple juice*   *orange juice*

lemonade   *pineapple slices*   *kiwi fruit*

banana

grapes   *lemon juice*

marshmallows

strawberries   *cherries*

1 To make the fruit punch, put the orange juice and the pineapple juice into ice-cube trays and freeze them until solid.

2 Mix together the tropical fruit juice and lemonade in a large jug. Put a mixture of the ice cubes in each glass and pour the fruit punch over. Decorate the glasses with the pineapple slices and cherries.

3 To make the fruit kebabs, thread 2 strawberries, 2 grapes, a marshmallow and a wedge of kiwi fruit onto each of twelve wooden skewers.

4 Peel the banana and cut it into twelve slices. Toss it in the lemon juice and thread the pieces onto the skewers. Serve immediately.

Citrus Cooler & Spicy Nuts

A knock-out of a cold drink for hot days, served with spicy nuts.

Serves 4

INGREDIENTS
FOR THE CITRUS COOLER
juice of 2 pink grapefruit
juice of 2 lemons
juice of 4 oranges
150 ml/¼ pint/⅔ cup
 pineapple juice
30 ml/2 tbsp caster
 (superfine) sugar
600 ml/1 pint/2½ cups lemonade
slices of lime and orange,
 to decorate

FOR THE SPICY NUTS
75 g/3 oz/⅓ cup butter
15 ml/1 tbsp oil
2 garlic cloves, crushed
30 ml/2 tbsp Worcestershire sauce
5 ml/1 tsp chili powder
5 ml/1 tsp ground turmeric
5 ml/1 tsp cayenne pepper
450 g/1 lb/4 cups mixed nuts

pink grapefruit

lemonade

pineapple juice

oranges

lemons

garlic

turmeric

butter

oil

Worcestershire sauce

chili powder

cayenne pepper

caster (superfine) sugar

mixed nuts

1 To make the citrus cooler, put the fruit juices in a large jug or bowl, stir in the sugar, then chill.

2 Add the lemonade and fruit slices, just before serving.

3 Make the nuts while the cooler is chilling. Heat the butter and oil in a frying pan until the butter melts. Stir in the garlic, Worcestershire sauce, spices and seasonings.

4 Cook gently for 1 minute, stirring all the time, then add the nuts and cook for 4–5 minutes, until lightly browned. Drain on paper towels and leave to cool before serving with the chilled drink.

Buck's Fizzy & Twizzles

Make the kids feel really sophisticated with this delicious alcohol-free version of a grown-up drink. Serve with savoury cheese twizzles.

Serves 6–8

INGREDIENTS
600 ml/1 pint/2½ cups fresh orange
   juice
45 ml/3 tbsp lemon juice
50 g/2 oz/½ cup icing
   (confectioners') sugar, sifted
300 ml/½ pint/1¼ cups bitter
   lemon, chilled
orange slices, to decorate

FOR THE TWIZZLES
225 g/8 oz/2 cups plain
   (all-purpose) flour
115 g/4 oz/½ cup butter,
   roughly chopped
15 ml/1 tbsp dried mixed herbs
50 g/2 oz mature (aged) Cheddar
   cheese, grated
cold water, to mix
salt and pepper

bitter lemon

flour

butter

water

cheese

**orange
slices**

**orange
juice**

pepper

**mixed
herbs**

**icing
(confectioners')
sugar**

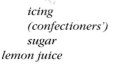
lemon juice

COOK'S TIP

Make some of the pastry strips into circles. After baking, slip three pastry strips inside each circle so each guests gets his or her personal set of twizzles.

1 To make the Buck's fizzy, mix the orange and lemon juice and the sugar in a jug (pitcher); stir and chill.

2 Just before serving, add the bitter lemon and decorate with orange slices.

3 Make the twizzles while the Buck's fizzy is chilling. Preheat the oven to 190°C/375°F/Gas 5. Put the flour and the butter in a bowl. Rub in the butter, then stir in the herbs, grated cheese and seasoning and add enough water to be able to pull the pastry together and knead it into a firm dough.

4 Roll out the dough until it is 5 mm/¼ in thick and cut it into 15 cm/ 6 in strips, about 1 cm/½ in wide. Twist each strip once or twice and arrange them in rows on a greased baking (cookie) sheet. Cook for 15–20 minutes, until golden brown. Cool the twizzles on a wire rack.

PARTY CAKES

For the grand finale of your party meal, turn off the lights and bring in one of these fantastic cakes with the candles blazing. A novelty cake makes a birthday celebration really special, and if you can keep it as a surprise for the birthday person until the moment you put it on the table, it will be even more exciting. All the decorating ideas in this chapter are based on square or round cakes, which are easy to make following our foolproof basic recipe. You'll be amazed at the brilliant shapes you can turn these into. We've used fondant icing, which you can make yourself or buy ready-made to save time. It's easy to mould and children love it.

Equipment

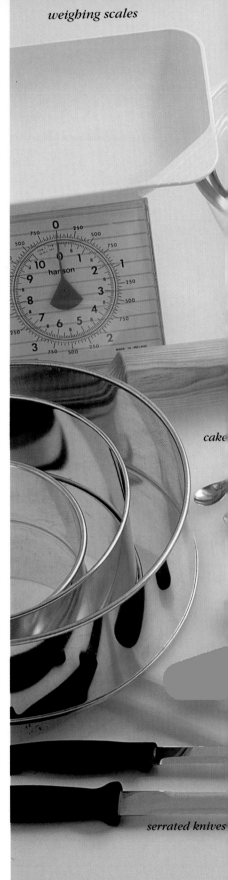

weighing scales

cake

serrated knives

Cake boards
Silver cake boards are perfect for presenting finished cakes. They come in a variety of shapes and sizes, in circles, squares and rectangles from 10 cm/4 in to 30 cm/12 in diameter.

Cake tins (pans)
All the cakes in this book use round or square tins (pans) in a variety of sizes. 15 cm/6 in, 20 cm/8 in and 25 cm/10 in are the most useful.

Electric hand-held beaters
These are real time-savers when mixing cake batters and icings.

Icing smoother
This will give a wonderfully smooth and uniform finish when spreading icing.

Measuring spoons
These are available in both metric and imperial measurements. Always measure level unless otherwise stated.

Mixing bowls
A set of various sizes is useful for mixing cake batters and icings.

Palette knives (metal spatulas)
These are useful for spreading butter icing onto cakes.

Pastry brush
This is essential for greasing cake tins (pans), and brushing cakes with apricot glaze.

Plastic chopping (cutting) board
Use this as a smooth, flat surface on which to roll fondant, if you do not have a suitable work surface to do this.

Plastic scrapers
These can be used to create all sorts of "combed" patterns in butter icing.

Rolling pin
Make sure you use a heavy rolling pin for rolling out marzipan and fondant.

Round cookie cutters
A set of cutters in various sizes can be used to create perfect rounds of fondant when making decorations.

Sable paintbrushes
These are expensive, but are well worth the extra cost when painting fine details onto cakes.

Serrated knives
Sharp knives with a serrated edge will allow you to cut cakes cleanly.

Sieves
Sieves are used for sifting flour into cake mixtures, for preparing icing (confectioners') sugar, and when making icing or dusting a surface before rolling out fondant.

Turntable
This enables you to turn the cake as you decorate which makes the task simpler.

Weighing scales
These are essential for accuracy when weighing ingredients, particularly for cakes.

Wooden toothpicks
These can be used to make designs on cakes, or to support pieces of cake to make a particular shape. If they are used as support, *always* remove them before serving.

Wooden spoons
A selection of wooden spoons is useful for stirring batters, icings and similar mixtures.

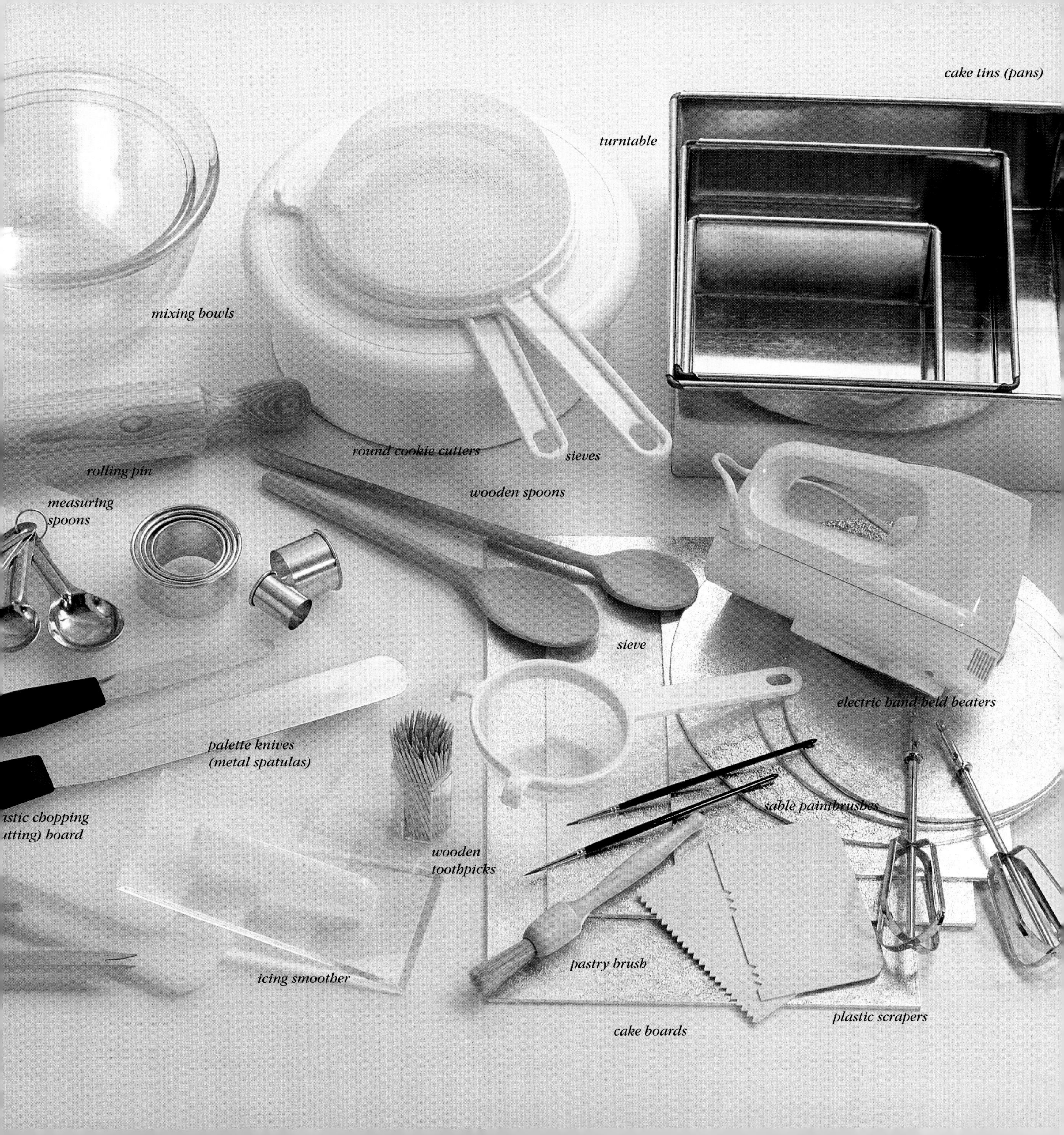

cake tins (pans)

turntable

mixing bowls

round cookie cutters

sieves

wooden spoons

rolling pin

measuring
spoons

sieve

electric hand-held beaters

palette knives
(metal spatulas)

sable paintbrushes

stic chopping
tting) board

wooden
toothpicks

icing smoother

pastry brush

plastic scrapers

cake boards

Cake Decorations

Cake decorating shops stock a variety of inexpensive, appealing items that can be used to enhance your cakes and enchant the children.

edible paste colours

numbers

flower cutters and ejecters

powder blossom tints

metal piping tubes

plastic train set

mini ribbon bows

novelties and toys

candles

sugar mouse

candle holders

cutters

Candles
A wide variety of shapes and colours are available from cake decorating shops and large department stores.

Candle holders
These are usually made of plastic, and come in various colours and sizes. They are available from both specialist suppliers and party shops.

Cutters
The varieties shown include a daisy flower cutter, a holly leaf cutter and a small flower cutter. They can be used for cutting fondant into specific shapes for decoration. These metal cutters can be purchased from specialist cake decorating shops and kitchenware suppliers.

Edible paste colours
These are very concentrated, so use them sparingly. They can be kneaded thoroughly into fondants to produce a bright and uniform colour.

A range of tools (left) and accessories for decorating party cakes. Specialist shops stock a variety of items, but you may also find suitable small novelties in toy shops.

Flower cutters with ejectors
These can be bought singly or in a boxed set with a small round sponge, and come in 5 mm (¼ in), 8 mm (⅜ in) and 1 cm (½ in) sizes. The ejector is on a spring, and the icing flowers are both cut and moulded by the tool, then pressed out of the cutter onto the sponge.

Metal piping tubes
These can be expensive, but it is worth investing in the best quality as they will produce lovely icing effects and will last for many years. The most useful ones to buy to start your collection are the no. 22 basket weave tube (a flat tube with a serrated edge); no. 1 writing tube (for writing, drawing outlines and producing run-out decorations); nos. 7 and 8 star tubes and no. 44 scroll tube for piping borders.

Mini ribbon bows
These make pretty additions to cakes and are bought in packs of 12, in all sorts of colours. Simply stick them into the icing.

Novelties and toys
You are likely to find a novelty to reflect almost any theme you choose in the better cake decorating shops. Illustrated here are plastic treble clefs, plastic miniature planes and plastic silver bells. The wooden sailing boat was purchased from a toy shop, another good source of small toys and novelties.

Plastic train set
This has a dual role as it also holds candles. The carriages are detachable so the correct number of candles may be used.

Powder blossom tints
These are edible dusting powders, which come in various colours and are used for brushing onto fondant icing to produce subtle shading. They can also be mixed to a paste with a product called "rejuvenator", which can be painted directly onto fondant. Both products are available from cake decorating shops.

Sugar mice
This example is home-made, and was made in a plastic mould with a string tail, but sugar animals can also be purchased from confectioners.

Lining a Cake Tin (Pan)

Careful lining is important to ensure that the cakes come out without breaking or sticking to the base of the tin (pan). This method is simple, but essential.

1 Place the tin (pan) on a piece of greaseproof (waxed) paper, draw around the base with a pencil and cut out the paper inside this line.

2 Grease the base and sides of the tin (pan) with melted butter or soft margarine. Stick the paper in neatly. Grease the paper. It is now ready for filling.

Apricot Glaze

This is used to seal the cake and stop any crumbs working their way into the icing. It will also stick the marzipan or fondant to the cake.

INGREDIENTS
175 g/6 oz/½ cup apricot jam
15 ml/1 tbsp water

1 Heat the apricot jam in a pan with the water, then rub through a sieve to remove any lumps. Return to the pan and heat until boiling before brushing carefully over the cake.

Basic Recipes

The recipes in this book all use simple round or square cake shapes. Make the cake to the required size, according to the chart on these pages.

For the lightest cakes, use polyunsaturated margarine. Margarine can be used straight from the fridge so all the ingredients can be put in a bowl and whisked together. There is no need to cream the fat and sugar first.

To make the required amount of butter icing, use the amount of sugar specified for the total weight of icing (for example, 350g/12 oz/2¾ cups butter icing requires 350 g/ 12 oz/2¾ cups sugar). Consult the chart to establish the proportions of butter and milk required for the weight of sugar.

Where a recipe calls for fondant or marzipan, you can use the shop-bought variety to save time, or make your own. For fondant, calculate the proportions as above (the total weight of fondant required is equal to the amount of sugar used). The marzipan recipe may be made in larger or smaller quantities as required. The royal icing recipe can also be made in smaller or larger batches, with the sugar used equal to the total weight called for in the recipe.

BASIC CAKE AND BUTTER ICING

15 cm/6 in round cake
2 eggs
115 g/4 oz/½ cup caster (superfine) sugar
115 g/4 oz/½ cup butter or margarine
115 g/4 oz/1 cup self raising (self-rising) flour
2.5 ml/½ tsp baking powder
15 ml/1 tbsp water

BUTTER ICING
15 g/½ oz/1 tbsp butter
7.5 ml/1½ tsp milk
50 g/2 oz/½ cup icing (confectioners') sugar, sifted

BAKING TIME
35–45 minutes

20 cm/8 in round cake
3 eggs
175 g/6 oz/¾ cup caster (superfine) sugar
175 g/6 oz/¾ cup butter or margarine
175 g/6 oz/1½ cups self raising (self-rising) flour
4 ml/¾ tsp baking powder
30 ml/2 tbsp water

BUTTER ICING
25 g/1 oz/2 tbsp butter
15 ml/1 tbsp milk
115 g/4 oz/1 cup icing (confectioners') sugar, sifted

BAKING TIME
45–55 minutes

25 cm/10 in round cake
6 eggs
350 g/12 oz/1½ cups caster (superfine) sugar
350 g/12 oz/1½ cups butter or margarine
350 g/12 oz/3 cups self raising (self-rising) flour
7.5 ml/1½ tsp baking powder
75 ml/5 tbsp water

BUTTER ICING
50 g/2 oz/¼ cup butter
30 ml/2 tbsp milk
225 g/8 oz/1½ cups icing (confectioners') sugar, sifted

BAKING TIME
1–1¼ hours

15 cm/6 in square cake
3 eggs
175 g/6 oz/¾ cup caster (superfine) sugar
175 g/6 oz/½ cup butter or margarine
175 g/6 oz/1½ cups self raising (self-rising) flour
4 ml/¾ tsp baking powder
30 ml/2 tbsp water

BUTTER ICING
15 g/½ oz/1 tbsp butter
7.5 ml/1½ tsp milk
50 g/2 oz/½ cup icing (confectioners') sugar, sifted

BAKING TIME
45–55 minutes

20 cm/8 in square cake
4 eggs
225 g/8 oz/1 cup caster (superfine) sugar
225 g/8 oz/1 cup butter or margarine
225 g/8 oz/2 cups self raising (self-rising) flour
5 ml/1 tsp baking powder
45 ml/3 tbsp water

BUTTER ICING
25 g/1 oz/2 tbsp butter
15 ml/1 tbsp milk
115 g/4 oz/1 cup icing (confectioners') sugar, sifted

BAKING TIME
50–60 minutes

25 cm/10 in square cake
8 eggs
450 g/1 lb/2 cups caster (superfine) sugar
450 g/1 lb/2 cups butter or margarine
450 g/1 lb/4 cups self raising (self-rising) flour
10 ml/2 tsp baking powder
105 ml/7 tbsp water

BUTTER ICING
50 g/2 oz/¼ cup butter
30 ml/2 tbsp milk
225 g/8 oz/1½ cups icing (confectioners') sugar, sifted

BAKING TIME
1½–1¾ hours

Basic Cake

All the designs that follow are based on this basic cake. Consult the chart for the correct proportions needed, and follow the simple steps below.

1 Preheat the oven to 190°C/375°F/ Gas 5. To grease and base line the cake tins (pans) you will be using, trace around the base on greaseproof (waxed) paper and cut out the circle. Grease the base and sides of the tin lightly with melted butter or margarine, then press the paper circle onto the bottom of the tin.

2 Put the eggs, sugar, margarine and flour into a bowl. Measure the baking powder level with a knife and add to the other ingredients in the bowl.

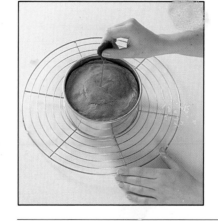

5 Bake in the centre of the oven for the time given in the chart, or until a thin skewer inserted into the centre of the cake comes out clean. Loosen the sides carefully with a knife. Cover a wire cooling rack with a piece of greaseproof paper (this will prevent the cake from sticking) and turn the cake onto the rack. Cool completely.

3 Whisk all the ingredients together until smooth and light.

4 Spoon into the prepared tin. Spread evenly to the sides.

TO MAKE BUTTER ICING

Soften the butter, add the milk and whisk in the sifted icing (confectioners') sugar until smooth. Add any flavouring and colouring required.

Marzipan

All the cakes in this book are covered with a layer of marzipan. It seals in the moisture and gives a smooth, flat surface on which to ice. It is easy to work with and useful for modelling. However, if your children do not like marzipan, replace it with a layer of fondant.

INGREDIENTS
225 g/8 oz/2 cups
    ground almonds
275 g/10 oz/1¼ cups caster
    (superfine) sugar
175 g/6 oz/1¼ cups icing
    (confectioners') sugar
1 egg
15–30 ml/1–2 tbsp lemon juice
3 ml/½ tsp almond extract

1 Mix all the dry ingredients in a bowl. Whisk the egg with the lemon juice and almond extract and add to the mixture in the bowl.

2 Mix together thoroughly and knead to form a smooth, pliable paste. Wrap in clear film until needed. Roll out on a work surface dusted with a little sifted icing (confectioners') sugar.

Royal Icing

This is used for piping, making run-out decorations and sticking decorations onto cakes. It dries very hard and holds its shape when piped.

INGREDIENTS
1 large egg white
225 g/8 oz/1½ cups icing
    (confectioners') sugar, sifted

COOK'S TIP

Dried egg white powder is available from supermarkets. It is whisked together with water and sifted icing (confectioners') sugar, following the manufacturers' instructions. Icing made this way must be covered at all times, as it dries very quickly.

1 Whisk the egg white in a large bowl with a fork. Add a quarter of the sugar and beat well.

2 Gradually work in the remaining sugar, beating well between each addition until the mixture holds its shape. Lay a piece of clear film (plastic wrap) on top of the icing and cover the bowl with a damp cloth to prevent the icing drying out. Store the mixture at room temperature.

Quick Fondant Icing

This can be bought or made at home. It is soft and pliable and must be worked with fairly quickly before it dries out. It should be wrapped in clear film (plastic wrap) if you are not using it immediately. Roll out on a smooth surface dusted with a little sifted icing (confectioners') sugar or cornflour (cornstarch). Fondant remains fairly soft for cutting and eating.

INGREDIENTS
500 g/1¼ lb/4½ cups icing
   (confectioners') sugar, sifted
1 large egg white
30 ml/2 tbsp liquid glucose
cornflour (cornstarch)

1 Put the icing (confectioners') sugar, egg white and liquid glucose into a food processor or mixer and blend until the mixture resembles fine breadcrumbs.

2 Knead the mixture with your hands until it becomes smooth and pliable, like dough. A drop of water may be added if the mixture is too dry. Add a little cornflour (cornstarch) if it is too sticky. The icing is ready when it no longer feels sticky and can be rolled out. (The whole process can be done by hand in a bowl.)

Gelatine Fondant Icing

This type of fondant icing is used for fine moulded decorations, as it dries very hard.

INGREDIENTS
60 ml/4 tbsp water
15 g/½ oz powdered gelatine
10 ml/2 tsp liquid glucose
500 g/1¼ lb/4½ cups icing
   (confectioners') sugar, sifted
cornflour (cornstarch)

1 Put the water in a heatproof bowl and sprinkle on the gelatine. Soak for 2 minutes. Place the bowl in a pan of hot but not boiling water and stir until the gelatine has dissolved and the liquid is clear. Remove from the pan and stir in the liquid glucose, then stir to cool.

2 Put the sugar into a bowl and mix in the gelatine mixture. Add more sugar or cornflour (cornstarch) if the mixture is too wet or a little water if it is too dry. Knead until smooth and pliable. Wrap in clear film (plastic wrap) until needed.

COLOURING FONDANT

Cake decorating shops sell a wide range of edible colours. Use only the thick paste colours to colour icing fondant, as liquid colours will make it too wet. Simply knead the paste thoroughly into the ready-made fondant. Coloured lustre powders are available to brush on after the icing has dried. Different effects can be achieved by applying the colours not only with a soft brush but with a sponge. A pale wash of colour can be painted on the icing and allowed to dry, then a fairly dry brush can be dragged across to give a "woodgrain" effect.

Making a Paper Piping Bag

Piping bags for icing are simple to make at home using greaseproof (waxed) paper. Make one for each colouring you will need and simply throw them away when you have finished.

1 Cut greaseproof (waxed) paper into a 25 cm (10 in) square. Fold in half diagonally to make a triangle. Fold again to mark the centre of the folded edge.

2 Holding the centre, roll one point of the triangle up to the central line and the other point around that to make a tight cone.

3 Fold the edges over tightly to secure the top of the bag.

Using a Piping Bag

Using a piping bag takes a little practice initially. It's best to try a few sample designs first.

1 Cut off the top of the bag, insert a piping tube and half-fill with royal icing.

2 Push the icing down well and fold both corners of the bag over to secure. Fold the top edge down several times until the icing is tightly packed in the bag.

3 Hold the bag in one hand and pipe in an upright position, guiding the bag with the other hand.

Making Run-out Decorations

These decorations can be piped onto the cake or onto a piece of greaseproof (waxed) paper which has been secured with masking tape to ensure that there are no creases. Draw the shapes onto the paper then pipe the outlines, which can then be "flooded" to fill the centre with a smooth, slightly domed surface. Always use freshly made royal icing.

1 Pipe the outline using a no. 1 writing tube, following the marks on the paper. Then slacken (thin) some icing with a drop of water. Be careful not to make the icing too runny or it will overflow the sides. If it is too thick, it will not give a smooth surface. You will have the correct consistency when the icing collapses and loses its shape if the bowl is tapped.

2 Half-fill a paper piping bag with soft icing, snip off a small hole and fill the outline shape generously to make the surface slightly domed. Use a pin to coax the icing into difficult areas and to break any bubbles as soon as they appear on the surface.

3 Allow the decorations to dry for at least 48 hours before peeling away the paper. Stick them on the cake with a little royal icing.

Making and Using Templates

Templates are a useful way of transferring a design from a book or drawing onto the surface of a cake. The designs you will need for the cakes shown are at the back of the book.

1 Place tracing or greaseproof (waxed) paper over the design to be copied and, using a sharp pencil, outline it neatly. If you are tracing a name, first draw a straight line on the paper with a ruler so that all the letters are even.

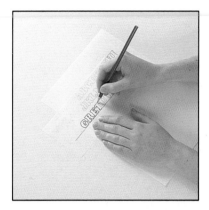

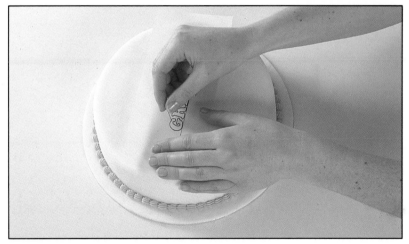

2 Turn the paper over and outline the design on the underside with a pencil. Turn the tracing the right way up and outline again onto the cake. A faint pencil outline will be transferred onto the cake. A more laborious method is to prick the design through the paper straight onto the cake using a pin.

3 Now the design can be piped over the outline to cover any marks.

Bella Bunny

This is an easy cake to make as the soft butter icing is simply spread all over the cake and the decoration does not require any special techniques.

INGREDIENTS
2 × 15 cm/6 in round cakes
350 g/12 oz/2¼ cups butter icing
apricot glaze
115 g/4 oz/2 cups dessicated (dry shredded) coconut
50 g/2 oz/¼ cup white fondant
food colourings: red and brown
marshmallows

EQUIPMENT
25 × 35.5 cm/10 × 14 in cake board
6 wooden toothpicks, stained brown with food colouring
candies

butter icing

apricot glaze

dessicated coconut

marshmallows

1 Split and fill the cakes with a little butter icing. Cut a 10 cm/4 in circle out of one cake and place both cakes on the cake board. Round off any sharp edges.

2 Use the trimmings to make the ears and feet.

3 Brush with hot apricot glaze. Cover with the remaining butter icing, then cover with coconut, pressing on lightly. Colour a piece of fondant ink and roll and shape the nose. Cut out oval shapes for the ears and put into place. Colour a small piece of fondant brown, roll two small balls for the eyes and put into place with the nose. Stick toothpicks on either side of the nose for whiskers. Push the candies into the marshmallows and place on the board around the cake.

The Teddy Bear's Birthday

This is an ideal design for a very young child's birthday. Draw a simple template that looks like the child's own bear.

INGREDIENTS
20 cm/8 in round cake
115 g/4 oz/³/₄ cup butter icing
apricot glaze
350 g/12 oz/2¹/₄ cups marzipan
450 g/1 lb/3 cups white fondant
food colourings: brown, red, blue
   and black
115 g/4 oz/³/₄ cup royal icing
silver balls

EQUIPMENT
25 cm/10 in round cake board
no. 7 star tube
no. 7 shell tube
1.5 mm/1³/₄ yards 2.5 cm/1 in wide
   ribbon
candles

apricot glaze

royal icing

fondant

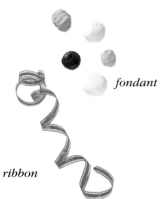
ribbon

1 Split and fill the cake with butter icing. Place on the cake board and brush with hot apricot glaze. Cover with marzipan, then with fondant. Using a template, mark the design on top of the cake.

2 Colour one-third of the remaining fondant pale brown. Colour a piece pink, a piece red, some blue and a tiny piece black. Using the template, cut out the pieces and place in position on the cake. Stick down by lifting the edges carefully and brushing the undersides with a little water. Roll small ovals for the eyes and stick in place with the nose and eyebrows. Cut out a mouth and press flat.

3 Tie the ribbon round the cake. Colour the royal icing blue and pipe the border around the base of the cake with the shell tube. Pipe tiny stars around the small cake with the star tube, inserting silver balls. Put the candles on the cake.

Hickory Dickory Dock

This appealing cake is based on the nursery rhyme. Small children love the clock's jolly face, and the sugar mouse can be given as a prize.

COOK'S TIP
You may want to model extra mice from pink fondant for the children to take home at the end of the party.

INGREDIENTS

20 cm/8 in round cake
15 cm/6 in square cake
225 g/8 oz/1½ cups butter icing
apricot glaze
675 g/1½ lb/4½ cups marzipan
450 g/1 lb/3 cups brown fondant
115 g/4 oz/¾ cup white fondant
food colourings: brown, gold, red, blue and black
2 silver balls
50 g/2 oz/¼ cup royal icing

EQUIPMENT

25 × 36 cm/ 10 × 14 in cake board
10 cm/4 in piece of string
no. 1 writing tube

apricot glaze

silver balls

fondant

1 Split and fill the cakes with butter icing. Cut two wedges off one end of the square cake, 6 cm/2½ in from the corner.

2 Use a cake tin (pan) as a guide to cut a semi-circle from the opposite end of the square cake to fit around the round cake. Place on the cake board and brush with hot apricot glaze. Cover with marzipan then with brown fondant.

3 Roll out half the white fondant and cut a 15 cm/6 in circle for the face and a window for the pendulum. Cut out a 5 cm/2 in long pendulum and 5 cm/2 in and 6 cm/2½ in long hands.

4 Paint the pendulum and hands gold and leave to dry overnight.

5 Colour most of the remaining fondant pink and make a mouse with a string tail and silver balls for eyes. Leave to dry overnight on greaseproof (waxed) paper.

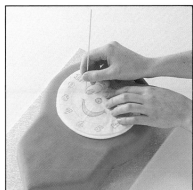

6 Stick on the clock face with a little water and use a template to mark the numbers and face. Pipe the outlines of the numbers, then colour some soft icing black and fill the centres. Stick on the window. Roll the excess brown fondant into long sausages and edge the face and the window. Colour the remaining fondant blue, red and black. Roll out and cut the eyes, pupils, eyebrows, mouth and centre. Use a little water to stick on the hands, features and pendulum. Stick on the mouse.

Noah's Ark

This charming cake is decorated with small purchased animals, about 4 cm/1½ in high, available from party and cake decorating shops. You could let the children choose one each to take home as a reminder of the party.

INGREDIENTS
20 cm/8 in square cake
115 g/4 oz/³⁄₄ cup butter icing
apricot glaze
450 g/1 lb/3 cups marzipan
450 g/1 lb/3 cups light brown
  fondant
115 g/4 oz/³⁄₄ cup royal icing
food colourings: brown, yellow and
  blue
chocolate mint stick

EQUIPMENT
25 cm/10 in square cake board
rice paper
small animal cake ornaments

royal icing

apricot glaze

animal ornaments

fondant

chocolate mint stick

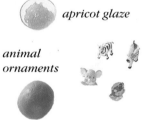

1 Split and fill the cake with butter icing. Cut a rectangle 20 x 13 cm/8 x 5 in and trim to shape the hull of the boat Place diagonally on the cake board.

2 Cut a smaller rectangle 10 x 6 cm/ 4 x 2½ in for the cabin and a triangular roof from the remaining piece of cake. Sandwich together with butter icing or apricot glaze.

3 Cover the three pieces with a layer of marzipan then cover the hull and cabin with brown fondant. Sandwich together with butter icing and place in position on the hull. Roll a long sausage from the remaining brown fondant and stick round the edge of the hull with a little water. Mark planks of wood with the back of a knife. Leave to dry overnight.

4 Colour one-third of the royal icing yellow and spread over the roof with a palette knife (spatula). Roughen it with a skewer to look like thatch.

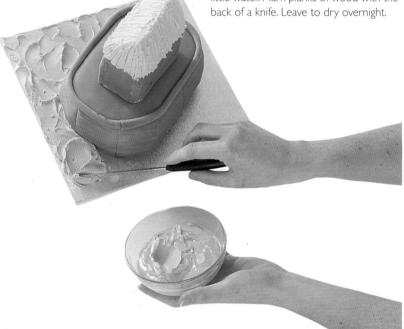

5 Colour the remaining royal icing blue and spread over the cake board, making rough waves. Stick a rice paper flag onto the chocolate mint stick and press on the back of the boat Stick the small animals onto the boat with dabs of icing.

Treasure Chest

Allow yourself a few days to make this cake. The lock and handles are made separately, then left to dry for 48 hours before sticking onto the cake.

INGREDIENTS
20 cm/8 in square cake
115 g/4 oz/³/₄ cup butter icing
apricot glaze
350 g/12 oz/2¹/₄ cups marzipan
350 g/12 oz/2¹/₄ cups brown fondant
50 g/2 oz/1 cup desiccated (dry shredded) coconut
115 g/4 oz/³/₄ cup royal icing
food colourings: brown, green and black
edible gold dusting powder
25 g/1 oz/3 tbsp white fondant
silver balls
chocolate coins

EQUIPMENT
30 cm/12 in round cake board

apricot glaze

silver balls

fondant

dessicated coconut

chocolate money

1 Split and fill the cake with butter icing. Cut the cake in half and sandwich the halves on top of each other. Place on the cake board.

2 Cut the top to shape the rounded lid and brush with hot apricot glaze. Cover with a layer of marzipan then a layer of brown fondant.

3 Mark the lid of the treasure chest with a sharp knife.

4 Lay strips of fondant over the chest to mark the panels.

5 Put the coconut in a bowl and mix in a few drops of green colouring. Spread a little royal icing over the cake board and press the "grass" lightly into it.

6 Cut out the padlock and handles. Cut a keyhole shape from the padlock and shape the handles over a small box. Leave to dry for 48 hours. Stick the padlock and handles into place with royal icing. Paint them gold and stick silver balls on the handles and padlock with a little royal icing to look like nails. Arrange the chocolate coins around the chest.

Treasure Map

Allow several days to paint the map because each colour must dry completely before adding another. Use a fairly dry paintbrush to apply the colour.

INGREDIENTS
25 cm/10 in square cake
225 g/8 oz/1½ cups butter icing
apricot glaze
450 g/1 lb/3 cups marzipan
450 g/1 lb/3 cups white fondant
225 g/8 oz/1½ cups yellow fondant
food colourings: yellow, brown,
  paprika, green, black and red
115 g/4 oz/¾ cup royal icing

EQUIPMENT
25 × 35 cm/10 × 14 in cake board
no. 7 shell tube
no. 1 writing tube
soft paintbrush

royal icing

apricot glaze

fondant

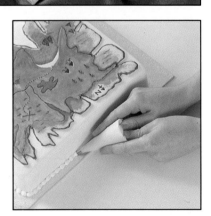

1 Split and fill the cake with butter icing. Cut into a 20 × 25 cm/8 × 10 in rectangle and place on the cake board. Brush with hot apricot glaze. Cover with a layer of marzipan then white fondant Roll out the yellow fondant and cut in an uneven outline. Stick onto the cake with water and dry overnight. Mark out an island, a river, a lake, mountains and trees on the map.

2 With brown and paprika colours and a fine paintbrush, paint the edges of the map to look old and smudge the colours together with a paper towel.

Paint the island pale green and the water around the island, river and lake pale blue. Dry overnight before painting on other details, otherwise the colours will run.

3 Pipe a border of royal icing around the base of the cake with a shell tube. Colour a little royal icing red and pipe the path to the treasure, marked with an "X". Colour some icing green and pipe on grass and trees. Colour some icing black and pipe on a "North" sign with a no. 1 tube.

Pirate's Hat

Black fondant is available ready-made from cake decorating shops. It is advisable to buy it rather than attempt to colour it black yourself.

INGREDIENTS
25 cm/10 in round cake
225 g/8 oz/1½ cups butter icing
apricot glaze
450 g/1 lb/3 cups marzipan
450 g/1 lb/3 cups black fondant
115 g/4 oz/¾ cup white fondant
food colourings: black and gold
chocolate coins
jewel sweets (candies)

EQUIPMENT
30 cm/12 in square cake board

apricot glaze

chocolate money

fondant

jewel sweets

1 Split and fill the cake with butter icing. Cut in half and sandwich the halves together. Stand upright diagonally across the cake board and use a template to cut shallow dips to create the crown of the hat. Brush with hot apricot glaze.

2 Cut a strip of marzipan to lay over the top of the cake to neaten the joints. Cover the whole cake with a layer of marzipan, then with black fondant.

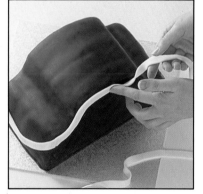

3 Roll out the white fondant and cut long strips 1 cm (½ in) wide. Use a little water to stick the strips in place around the brim of the hat.

4 Mark the strip with a fork to look like braid. With a template, mark the skull and cross bones onto the hat. Cut the shapes out of the white fondant and stick in place with a little water. Paint the braid strip around the hat gold and arrange the chocolate coins and jewel sweets (candies) around the board.

Spider's Web

Make the marzipan spider several days before you need the cake to give it time to dry. It is important to get the consistency of the glacé icing right; you can practise by pouring some icing onto a baking (cookie) sheet and piping on the web.

INGREDIENTS
20 cm/8 in round cake
225 g/8 oz/1½ cups butter icing
apricot glaze
30 ml/2 tbsp cocoa
chocolate vermicelli (sprinkles)
40 g/1½ oz/4 tbsp yellow marzipan
food colourings: red and brown
225 g/8 oz/1½ cups icing
   (confectioners') sugar
15–30 ml/1–2 tbsp water

EQUIPMENT
25 cm/10 in round cake board
wooden toothpick
star tube
candles

butter icing

apricot glaze

marzipan

chocolate vermicelli

1 Split and fill the cake with half the butter icing. Brush the sides with hot apricot glaze. Add cocoa to the remaining butter icing, smooth a little over the sides (reserve the rest) and roll the sides of the cake in chocolate vermicelli (sprinkles). Place on a board.

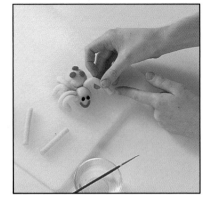

2 To make the spider, roll 25 g/1 oz/ 2 tbsp of the yellow marzipan into two balls for the body and thorax. Colour a small piece of marzipan red and roll into small dots, then stick them onto the back. Divide the rest of the marzipan into eight pieces and roll into legs 5 cm/2 in long. Stick into place and leave to dry on greaseproof (waxed) paper. Make brown eyes and a red mouth and stick in place.

3 Next make the spider's web. The glacé icing sets quickly, so have everything ready. Sift the sugar into a bowl, then gradually beat in the water. Place the bowl in a pan with hot, but not boiling, water. Heat gently and stir the icing; it should coat the back of the spoon. If the icing is too thick add a drop of water and if it is too thin add a little more sifted sugar. (Be careful not to overheat the icing.) Remove from the pan, dry the bowl and quickly pour two-thirds of the icing over the top of the cake. Spread to the edges with a palette knife (spatula). Tap the cake firmly on the work surface to flatten the icing.

4 Add a drop of brown colouring to the remaining glacé icing and pour into a piping bag. Snip a tiny hole off the end and pipe a spiral onto the cake, starting from the centre and working outwards.

With a wooden toothpick draw across the cake from the centre outwards, dividing it into quarters. Then divide each quarter in half, to complete the web. Leave to set.

5 Put the rest of the chocolate butter icing into a piping bag fitted with a star tube and pipe a border around the edge of the web. Put candles evenly around the border and the spider in the centre.

Frog Prince

This cake needs some preparation in advance, as the crown takes 48 hours to dry.

INGREDIENTS
20 cm/8 in round cake
115 g/4 oz/³/₄ cup butter icing
apricot glaze
450 g/1 lb/3 cups marzipan
450 g/1 lb/3 cups green fondant
115 g/4 oz/³/₄ cup royal icing
50 g/2 oz/¹/₄ cup white fondant
food colourings: green, red, black and gold
cornflour (cornstarch), for dusting

EQUIPMENT
25 cm/10 in square cake board
paintbrush

apricot glaze

fondant

1 Split and fill the cake with butter icing. Cut it in half and sandwich both halves together with apricot glaze. Stand upright diagonally across the cake board.

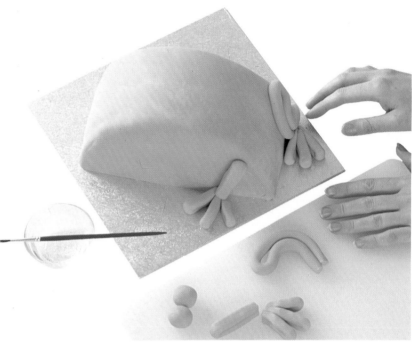

2 Brush the cake with hot apricot glaze. Cover with a layer of marzipan, then with green fondant. To make the legs and feet, roll green fondant into 20 cm/8 in lengths about 1 cm/½ in in diameter. Fold in half for the back legs and stick on with a little water. The front legs are rolled into 10 cm/4 in lengths, folded in half and pinched to taper to the foot end. The feet are made in the same way, cut to 4 cm/1½ in lengths and pinched together to tapered ends. Stick in place with a little royal icing. Roll balls for the eyes and stick in place on top of the cake.

3 Roll out the white fondant. Cut a strip 5 × 19 cm/2 × 7½ in and mark one edge at 2.5 cm/1 in intervals then cut out triangles to make the crown shape. Wrap around a glass dusted with cornflour (cornstarch) and moisten the edges to join. Leave to dry (this may take up to 48 hours). Cut a 10 cm/4 in circle for the white shirt. Stick in place and trim the edge level with the cake board. Cut white circles and stick to the eyes. Colour a little fondant pink, roll into a sausage and stick on for the mouth. Colour a little fondant black, roll out and cut pupils for the eyes and bow tie and stick in place.

4 Paint the crown gold and stick into position with royal icing.

Happy Monkey

This cheeky little monkey can be made in any colour fondant you wish.

INGREDIENTS
20 cm/8 in round cake
115 g/4 oz/³/₄ cup butter icing
apricot glaze
450 g/1 lb/3 cups marzipan
450 g/1 lb/3 cups pink fondant
50 g/2 oz/¹/₄ cup white fondant
food colourings: pink, blue and
  black

EQUIPMENT
25 cm/10 in round cake board
candles

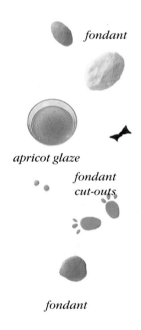

fondant

apricot glaze

*fondant
cut-outs*

fondant

1 Split and fill the cake with butter icing. Place on the cake board and, with a sharp serrated knife, use the template to cut out the basic shape of the monkey. Use the trimmings to shape the nose and tummy. Brush with hot apricot glaze and cover with a layer of marzipan then pink fondant. Leave to dry overnight.

2 Mark the position of the paws and face. Colour a little of the fondant blue, roll out and cut out the eyes. Colour a little fondant black and cut out the pupils and tie.

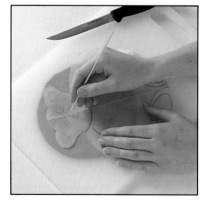

3 Colour the remaining fondant pink and cut out the paws, nose, mouth and ears. Stick the features in place with water. Roll the trimmings into two balls and place on the board for the candles.

Drum

If your birthday party has a musical theme, this is a very easy and colourful way to decorate a circular cake. It will appeal to young children.

INGREDIENTS
15 cm/6 in round cake
50 g/2 oz/¼ cup butter icing
apricot glaze
350 g/12 oz/2¼ cups marzipan
450 g/1 lb/3 cups white fondant
food colourings: red, blue and
  yellow

EQUIPMENT
20 cm/8 in round cake board

marzipan

apricot glaze

butter icing

fondant

COOK'S TIP
If you don't have time to allow fondant drumsticks to dry out, use candy sticks instead.

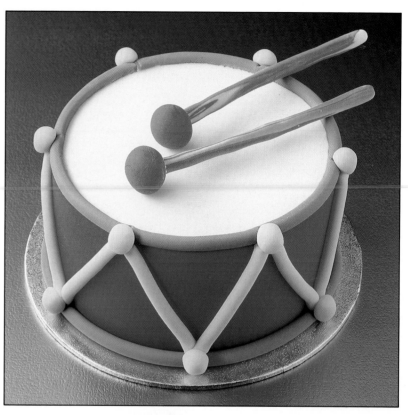

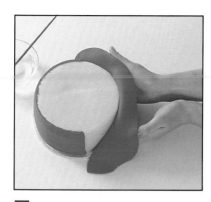

1 Split and fill the cake with a little butter icing. Place on the cake board and brush with hot apricot glaze. Cover with a layer of marzipan and leave to dry overnight. Colour half the fondant red. Roll out to 25 × 30 cm/10 × 12 in and cut in half. Stick to the sides of the cake with water, smoothing the joins neatly.

2 Roll out a circle of white fondant to fit the top of the cake and divide the rest in half. Colour one half blue and the other yellow. Divide the blue into four equal pieces and roll each piece into a sausage long enough to go half way round the cake. Stick around the base and top of the cake with a little water.

3 Mark the cake into six around the top and bottom using greaseproof (waxed) paper marked in six wedges.

4 Roll most of the yellow fondant into strands long enough to cross diagonally from top to bottom to form the drum strings. Roll the rest of the yellow fondant into 12 small balls and stick where the strings join the drum. Using red and white fondant knead together until streaky and roll two balls and sticks 15 cm/6 in long. Dry overnight. Stick together with butter icing to make the drumsticks and place on top.

Clown Face

Children love this happy clown. His frilly collar is quite easy to make, but you do have to work quickly before the fondant dries.

INGREDIENTS
20 cm/8 in round cake
115 g/4 oz/³/₄ cup butter icing
apricot glaze
450 g/1 lb/3 cups marzipan
450 g/1 lb/3 cups white fondant
115 g/4 oz/³/₄ cup royal icing
food colourings: pink, red, green, blue and black
silver balls

EQUIPMENT
25 cm/10 in round cake board
no. 8 star tube
fluted circular cutter
small circular cutter
wooden skewer
cotton wool (balls)
candles

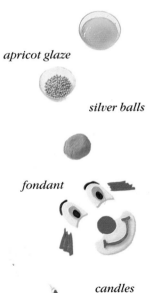

apricot glaze

silver balls

fondant

candles

1 Split and fill the cake with butter icing. Place in the centre of the cake board and brush with hot apricot glaze. Cover with a thin layer of marzipan, then white fondant. Mark the position of the features. Pipe stars around the base of the cake with royal icing, placing silver balls as you work, and leave to dry overnight.

2 Colour half the remaining fondant pale pink, roll out and with the use of a template, cut out the shape of the face. Lay on the cake with the top of the head touching one edge of the cake.

3 Colour the remaining pink fondant red, roll out and cut out the nose. Roll out some of the white fondant, cut out the eyes and mouth and stick on the face with the nose, using a little water. Roll out a little of the red fondant into a thin sausage and cut to fit the mouth. Stick in place with a little water.

4 Roll out the rest of the red fondant, cut in thin strands for hair and stick in place with water.

5 Colour most of the remaining fondant pale green and roll out thinly. Cut out a fluted circle with a small plain inner circle. Cut through one side and roll along the fluted edge with a wooden skewer to stretch it. Stick on the cake with a little water and arrange the frills.

6 Repeat to make three layers of frills, supporting them with cotton wool (balls) until dry. Colour a little fondant blue, roll and cut out eyes and stick in place with a little water. Colour the rest of the fondant black, roll and cut out the pupils and eye brows, then stick in position. Place the candles at the top of the head.

Balloons

This is a simple yet effective design that can be adapted to any age. Young children like it especially.

INGREDIENTS
20 cm/8 in round cake
115 g/4 oz/³/₄ cup butter icing
apricot glaze
450 g/1 lb/3 cups marzipan
450 g/1 lb/3 cups white fondant
food colourings: pink, blue, green and yellow
100 g/4 oz/³/₄ cup royal icing

EQUIPMENT
25 cm/10 in cake board
1.5 m/1³/₄ yards 4cm/1¹/₂ in wide ribbon
no. 2 plain tube
no. 7 star tube
candies

apricot glaze

fondant

ribbon

1 Split and fill the cake with butter icing. Place on the cake board and brush with hot apricot glaze. Cover with a layer of marzipan, then with white fondant. Divide the remaining fondant into three pieces; colour one pink, one blue and the other green. Roll out and, using a template, cut out a balloon from each colour. Stick onto the cake with a little water, rubbing the edges gently with a finger to round them off.

2 Tie the ribbon round the cake. With yellow royal icing and a plain tube, pipe on the strings, attaching them to the balloons. Pipe a border around the base of the cake.

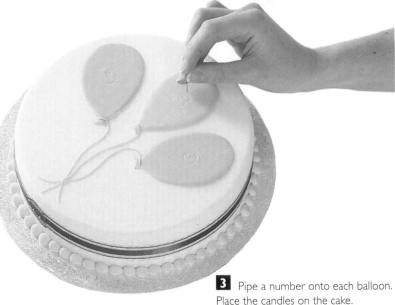

3 Pipe a number onto each balloon. Place the candles on the cake.

Toy Car

This little car can be made for any age. You could add a personalized number (license) plate with the child's name and age to the back of the car.

INGREDIENTS
20 cm/8 in round cake
115 g/4 oz/³/₄ cup butter icing
apricot glaze
450 g/1 lb/3 cups marzipan
450 g/1 lb/3 cups yellow fondant
50 g/2 oz/¹/₄ cup red fondant
food colourings: yellow, red and
   black
30 ml/2 tbsp royal icing
sweets (candies)

EQUIPMENT
25 cm/10 in round cake board
4 cm/1¹/₂ in and 2.5 cm/1 in plain
   circle cutters
no. 1 writing tube
candles

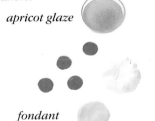

apricot glaze

fondant

sweets

1 Split and fill the cake with a little butter icing. Cut in half and sandwich the halves upright together. With a sharp serrated knife, cut a shallow dip to shape the front of the car. Place on the cake board and brush with hot apricot glaze. Cut a strip of marzipan level to the joins on top of the cake. Then cover with a layer of marzipan and a layer of yellow fondant. Leave to dry overnight.

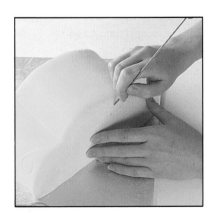

2 Mark the doors and windows on the car with a sharp skewer.

3 Roll out the red fondant and cut out four 4 cm/1¹/₂ in wheels with a cutter. Stick in place with a little water. Mark the centre of each wheel with a smaller cutter. Colour the royal icing black and pipe over the doors and windows. Stick on sweets (candies) for headlights with a little royal icing. Press the candles into sweets and stick to the board with a little royal icing.

Dart Board

Start the decoration several days beforehand, as lots of patience and time is required. Once the cake is covered with marzipan and fondant, the decoration can be worked on in stages.

INGREDIENTS

25 cm/10 in round cake
175 g/6 oz/scant cup butter icing
apricot glaze
450 g/1 lb/3 cups marzipan
450 g/1 lb/3 cups black fondant
115 g/4 oz/³/₄ cup yellow fondant
10 g/¹/₄ oz/1 tsp red fondant
115 g/4 oz/³/₄ cup royal icing
food colourings: black, yellow, red
    and silver

EQUIPMENT

30 cm/12 in round cake board
1 cm/¹/₂ in plain circle cutter
no. 1 writing tube
paintbrush
candles

apricot glaze

fondant

1 Split and fill the cake with butter icing. Put onto the cake board and brush with hot apricot glaze. Cover with a layer of marzipan then black fondant. Wrap the rest in clear film (plastic wrap) until needed. Make a template to mark the board into equal sections. Draw a 20 cm/8 in circle onto a piece of greaseproof (waxed) paper, cut out and fold in quarters. Mark each quarter into five equal portions and draw in lines to meet in the centre. Place the template on the cake and mark the centre and the edge of each wedge onto the cake.

2 Mark the wedges on the top of the cake with a sharp knife. Roll out the yellow fondant and cut out wedges using the template as a guide. Place on alternate sections but do not stick in place yet. Repeat with the rest of the black fondant.

3 Carefully cut 3 mm/⅛ in off each wedge and swap the colours. Mark a 13 cm/5 in circle in the centre of the board and cut out 3 mm/⅛ in pieces to swap with adjoining colours. Stick in place and use an icing smoother to flatten.

4 Use the cutter to remove the centre for the bull's eye. Cut out and stick on a red fondant bull's eye and surround with a thin strip of black fondant. Roll the remaining black fondant into a long sausage to fit around the base of the cake and stick in place using a little water.

5 Mark numbers onto the board and pipe on with royal icing using a no. 1 tube. Leave to dry then paint the numbers with silver. Stick candles into the cake at an angle to resemble darts.

Space Ship

For this cake, the triangles for the jets should be covered with marzipan and fondant separately, then stuck into position after decorating.

INGREDIENTS
25 cm/10 in square cake
225 g/8 oz/1½ cups butter icing
apricot glaze
350 g/12 oz/2¼ cups marzipan
450 g/1 lb/3 cups white fondant
food colourings: blue, pink and
black

EQUIPMENT
30 cm/12 in square cake board
candles
gold paper stars

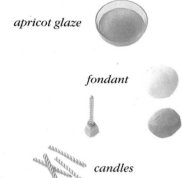

apricot glaze

fondant

candles

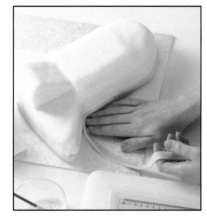

1 Split and fill the cake with a little butter icing. With a sharp serrated knife, cut a piece 10 cm/4 in wide diagonally across the middle of the cake. Cut straight across one end, so that the space ship is about 25 cm/10 in long.

2 Shape the nose and cut the remaining cake in three 7.5 cm/3 in triangles for the sides and top of the ship. Cut two smaller triangles for the boosters and trim any remaining cake to fit down the middle of the space ship. Assemble diagonally across the cake board and brush with hot apricot glaze. Cover with a layer of half of the marzipan, then with white fondant.

3 Colour one-third of the remaining fondant blue, one-third pink and one-third black. Wrap each separately in clear film (plastic wrap). Roll out the blue and cut in 1 cm/½ in strips. Stick in a continuous line around the base with a little water and outline the triangles. Cut a 2.5 cm/1 in strip and stick down the centre of the ship.

4 Roll out the pink fondant and cut out shapes to decorate the ship. Roll out the black fondant and cut out windows, circles, name and numbers. Stick in place with a little water.

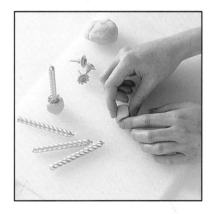

5 With any leftover fondant, make candle holders by shaping into small cubes. Stick the candles into them, then stick onto the board. Decorate the board with gold stars.

Fairy

This cake would enchant many little girls, but requires skill and patience. Allow plenty of time if you are trying the techniques for the first time.

INGREDIENTS
20 cm/8 in round cake
115 g/4 oz/³/₄ cup butter icing
apricot glaze
450 g/1 lb/3 cups marzipan
400 g/14 oz/2³/₄ cups pale blue fondant
50 g/2 oz/¹/₄ cup white fondant
food colourings: blue, pink, yellow and gold
115 g/4 oz/¹/₂ cup royal icing
silver balls

EQUIPMENT
25 cm/10 in cake board
no. 1 writing tube
fine paintbrush
pink sparkle lustre powder
fluted circle cutter
small plain circle cutter
wooden skewer
cotton wool (balls)
no. 7 star tube
silver ribbon

fondant

silver balls

lustre powder

royal icing

silver ribbon

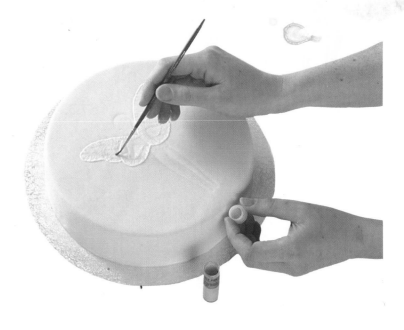

1 Split and fill the cake with butter icing. Place on the board and brush with hot apricot glaze. Cover with a thin layer of marzipan, then with pale blue fondant. Leave to dry overnight. Using a template, carefully mark the position of the fairy onto the cake. As royal icing dries quickly, work only on about 2.5 cm/1 in sections of the fairy's wings at a time. Fill a piping bag with a no. 1 tube with white royal icing and carefully pipe over the outline of each wing section.

2 Pipe a second line just inside that and, with a damp paintbrush, brush long strokes from the edges towards the centre, leaving more icing at the edges and fading away to a thin film near the base of the wings. Leave to dry for 1 hour. Brush with dry lustre powder (not dissolved in spirit).

3 Colour a little fondant flesh colour, roll and cut out the body. Lay carefully in position. Dampen a paintbrush, remove the excess water on a paper towel and carefully brush under the arms, legs and head to stick. Round off any sharp edges by rubbing gently with a finger. Cut out the bodice and shoes and stick in place. Cut out a wand and star and leave to dry.

4 Work quickly to make the tutu, as thin fondant dries quickly and will crack easily. Each frill must be made separately. Roll out a small piece of fondant to 3 mm/⅛ in thick and cut out a fluted circle with a small plain inner circle. (The depth of the frill will be governed by the size of the central hole; the smaller the central hole, the wider the frill.)

5 Cut into quarters and, with a wooden skewer, roll along the fluted edge to stretch it and produce fullness.

6 Attach the frills to the waist with a little water. Repeat with the other layers, tucking the sides under neatly. Use a wooden skewer to arrange the frills and small pieces of cotton wool (balls) to hold the folds of the skirt in place until dry. Leave to dry overnight. Brush a little lustre powder over the edge of the tutu. Paint on the hair and face, stick on the wand and star and paint the star gold. Pipe a border of royal icing round the edge of the board with a star nozzle and place silver balls on alternate points. Leave to dry. Colour a little royal icing yellow and pipe over the hair. Paint with a touch of gold colouring.

TEMPLATES

Some of the projects in this book need templates. You can either trace them directly from the book, or enlarge them to the size required.

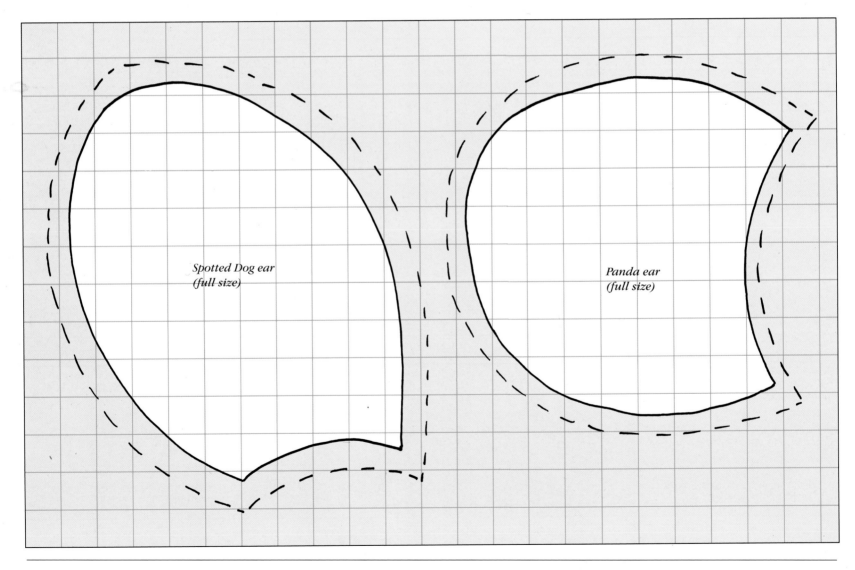

Spotted Dog ear (full size)

Panda ear (full size)

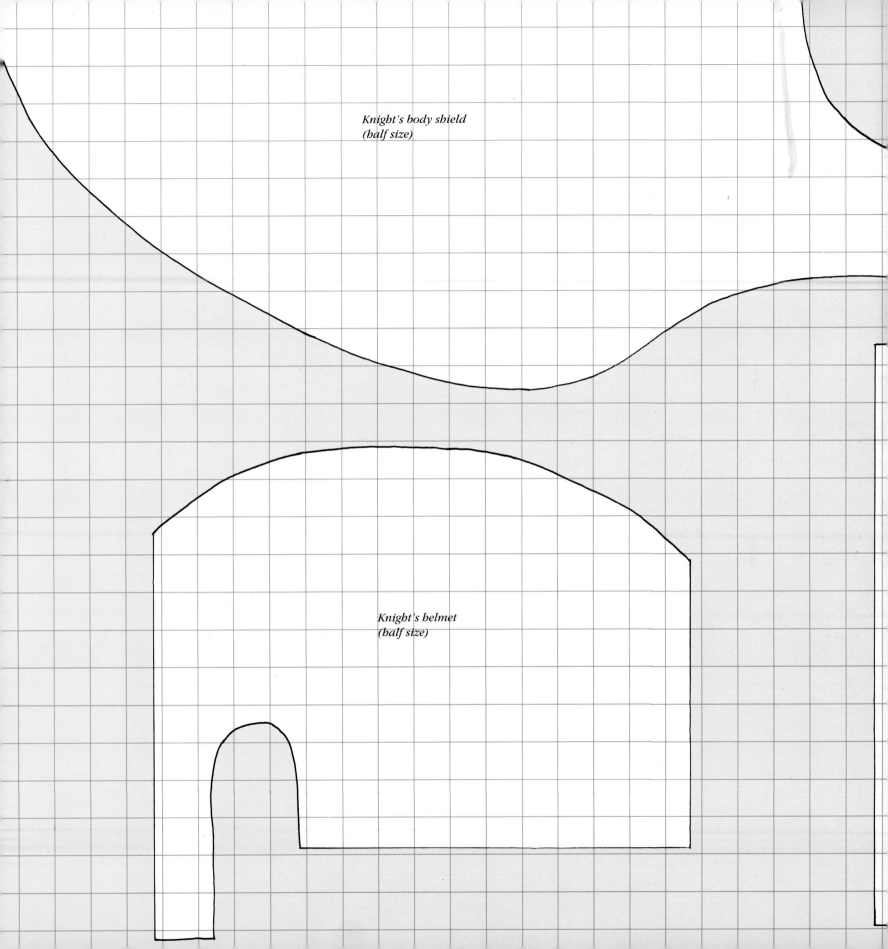

Knight's body shield
(half size)

Knight's helmet
(half size)

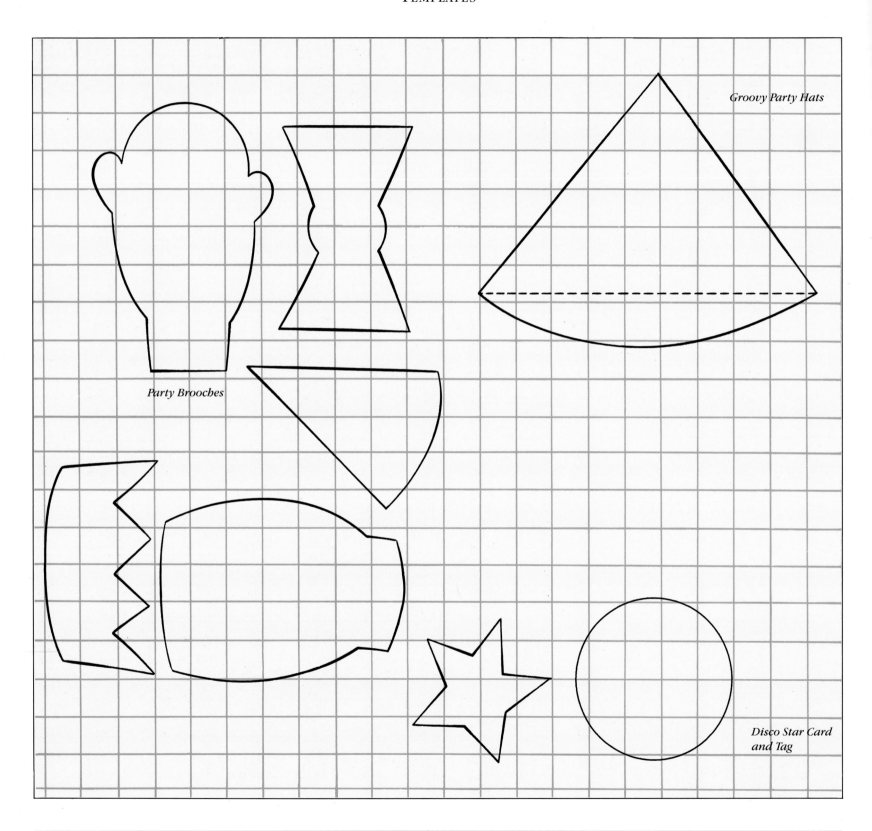

Groovy Party Hats

Party Brooches

Disco Star Card
and Tag

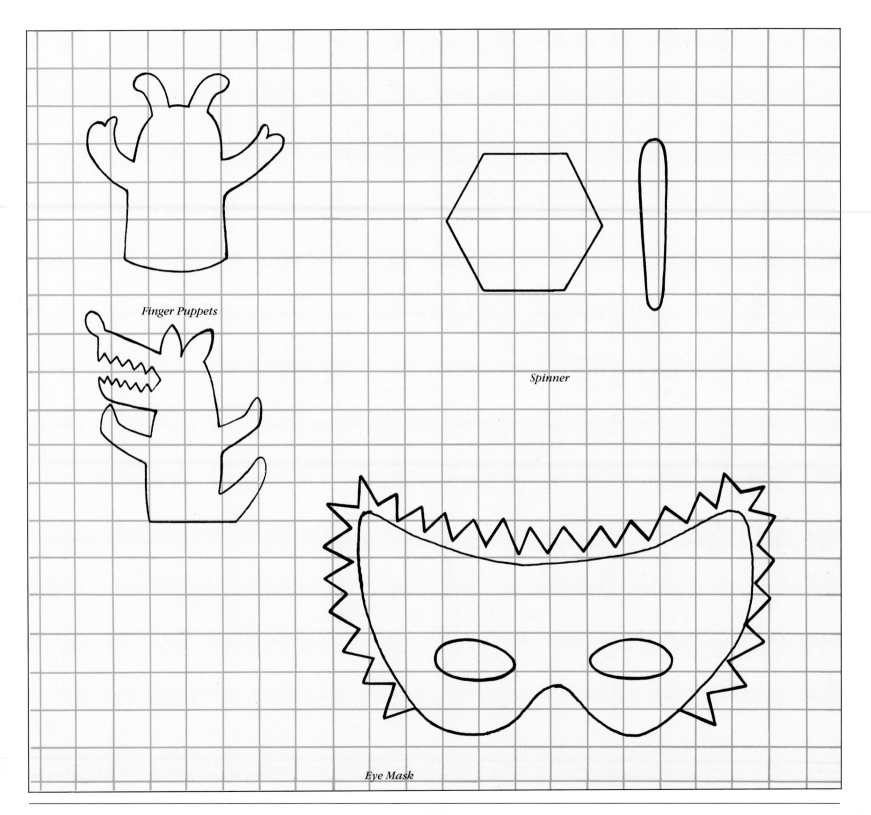

Finger Puppets

Spinner

Eye Mask

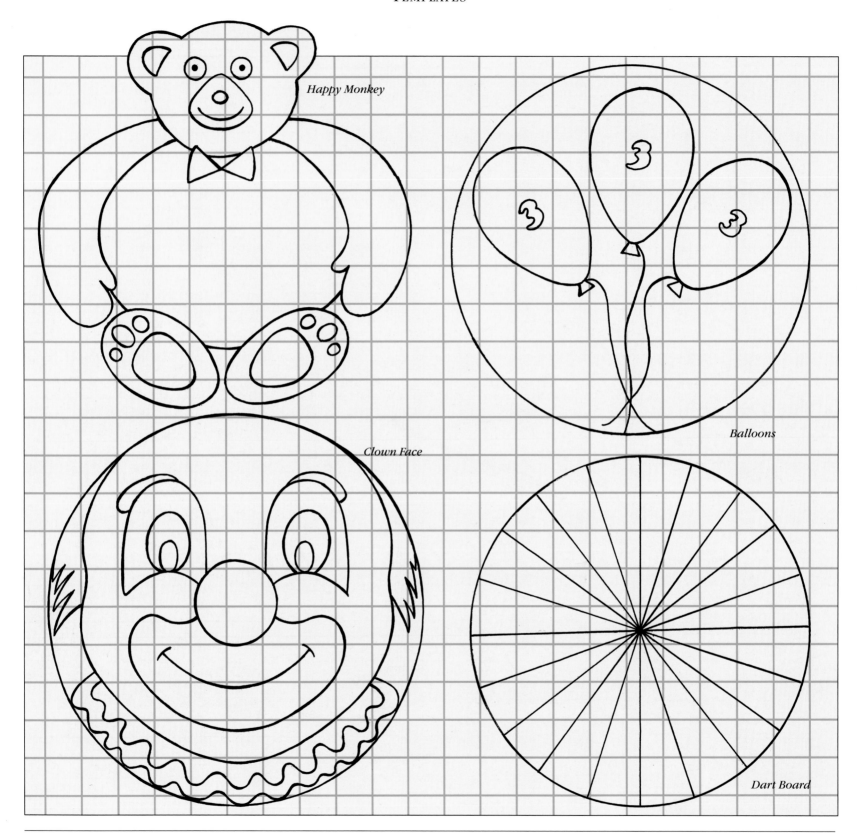

Happy Monkey

Balloons

Clown Face

Dart Board

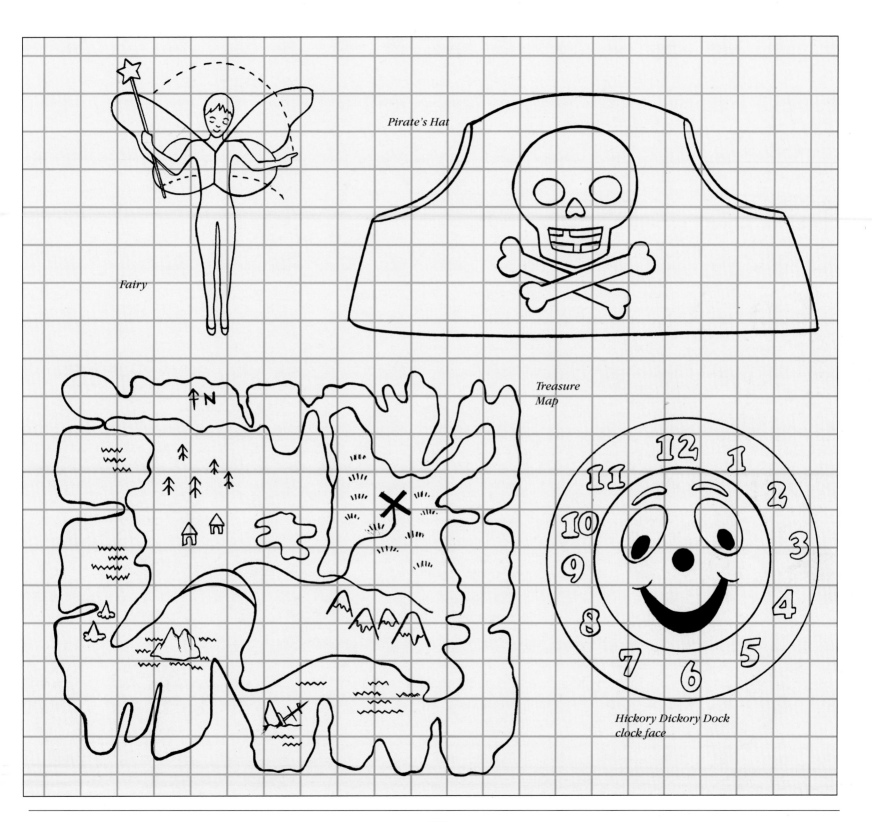

Fairy

Pirate's Hat

Treasure
Map

Hickory Dickory Dock
clock face

INDEX

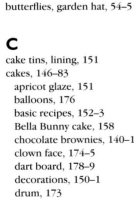

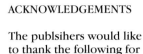

ACKNOWLEDGEMENTS

The publsihers would like to thank the following for their contribution to this project:

Beverley Jollands for writing the introduction and editing this book.

Additional projects by:
Nick Huckleberry Beak, Marion Elliot, Sara Lewis, Sally Walton and Judy Williams.

Photographers:
Edward Allwright, James Duncan, John Freeman, Michelle Garrett, David Jordan, Mark Wood and Polly Wreford.

Stylists:
Petra Boase, Susan Bull and mria kelly.

Face Painting by Bettina Graham.